For P.

With thanks to Derek John and all those at Frances Lincoln
who helped and advised me as I worked on this book.

The Publishers would like to thank Derek John ARIBA
for acting as the consultant for this book.

The Picture History of Great Buildings copyright © Frances Lincoln Limited 2007
Text and illustrations copyright © Gillian Clements 2007

First published in Great Britain in 2007 and in the USA in 2008 by
Frances Lincoln Children's Books, 4 Torriano Mews,
Torriano Avenue, London NW5 2RZ

www.franceslincoln.com

British Library Cataloguing in Publication Data available on request

ISBN: 978-1-84507-488-3

The illustrations for this book are watercolour

Printed in Singapore

1 3 5 7 9 8 6 4 2

THE PICTURE HISTORY OF
GREAT BUILDINGS

GILLIAN CLEMENTS

F

FRANCES LINCOLN
CHILDREN'S BOOKS

Contents

Introduction 7

The First Homes 8

The First Cities 9

Ancient Monuments 10

The Step Pyramid 12

The Parthenon 13

The Colosseum 14

Hagia Sophia 15

The Great Mosque 16

Angkor Wat 17

Romanesque 18

Gothic 19

Amiens Cathedral 20

Palazzo Vecchio 21

The Renaissance in Italy 22

St Peter's Basilica 24

Villa Rotonda 25

St Basil's Cathedral 26

The Globe 27

Temple Mayor 28

Baroque and Rococo 30

St Peter's Piazza 32

The Palace of Versailles 33

St Paul's Cathedral 34

Taj Mahal 35

The Enlightenment 36

Romantic and Revolutionary 37

Houses of Parliament 38

Paris Opéra House 39

Changing Cities 40

Iron and the Industrial Age 42

Brooklyn Bridge 44

Eiffel Tower 45

New York's First Skyscrapers 46

Chicago's First Skyscrapers 47

Sagrada Familia 48

The Bauhaus 49

The Chrysler Building 50

Unité D'Habitation 51

Guggenheim Museum 52

The Sydney Opera House 53

World High Rises 54

Postmodern Buildings 56

Contemporary and Beyond 57

Glossary 58

Index 60

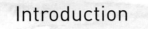

Introduction

Long ago, people built their homes and shelters out of natural materials. There were no great buildings, just a roof over the head – protection from weather and a harsh environment.

Centuries passed. Most hunter-gatherers abandoned their nomadic lifestyles to build houses, and in time, towns. Cities grew. Men who had acquired exceptional building skills began designing great monuments, like the ziggurats of the Fertile Crescent (now Iraq), and the pyramids of Ancient Egypt.

Throughout history, religion and culture have often been the driving forces behind architects' and engineers' greatest buildings. From the 19th century, technology and new materials have given architects the ability to design breathtaking buildings – structures that even reach to the sky.

But what of the future? Perhaps now is the time to build 'green' homes and workplaces that work in harmony with our fragile climate.

In the meantime, I hope this book tells the entertaining story of some of our world's greatest Great Buildings.

Gillian Clements

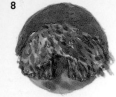

THE FIRST HOMES

In prehistoric times, people used whatever they could find to make shelters for themselves against the weather. They made these homes from wood, stone, mud, reeds and even animal skins and bones. If they were lucky they lived in caves.

People first built simple shelters about 12,000 years ago, changing and perfecting them over many generations. Some people still build homes like this today, following in the footsteps of their ancestors.

Paintings found on the walls of caves in southern France are believed to be 20,000 years old.

Huts in Mesopotamia were made from marshland reeds which kept them cool in the warm weather.

Mud from rivers (sun-dried or fired to make bricks) was an ideal building material. A protective skin of fired bricks, plaster or limewash covered important buildings.

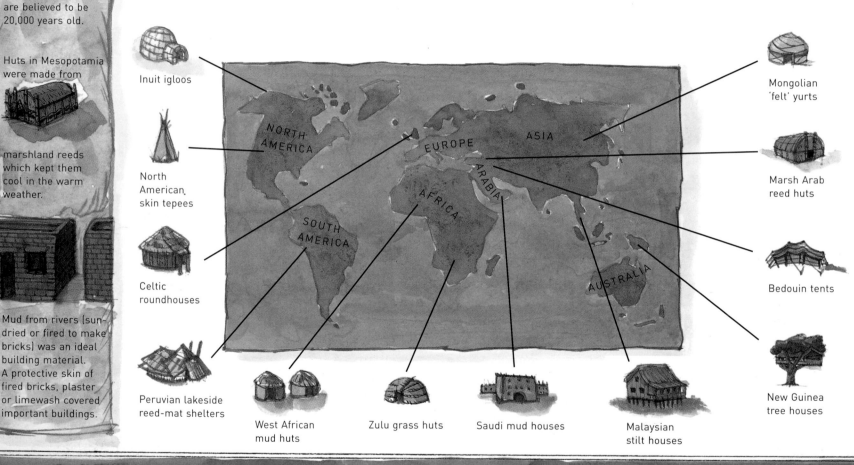

Inuit igloos

North American skin tepees

Celtic roundhouses

Peruvian lakeside reed-mat shelters

West African mud huts

Zulu grass huts

Saudi mud houses

Malaysian stilt houses

Mongolian 'felt' yurts

Marsh Arab reed huts

Bedouin tents

New Guinea tree houses

NORTH AMERICA

SOUTH AMERICA

EUROPE

ASIA

AFRICA

ARABIA

AUSTRALIA

The first buildings were simple shelters made from natural materials.

Jericho

1 million years ago Neanderthal people make clothes from skins and live in caves.

100,000–35,000 years ago Modern humans survive the Ice Age by living in caves and hunting.

8300 BC After the great Ice Age, there are new continents. Farming begins to develop.

8000 BC Jericho, near the Dead Sea, is one of the earliest villages.

6000 BC People use a wheel to make pottery and copper instead of stone to make strong tools.

THE FIRST CITIES
From 5000 BC

Jerico's stone walls were built over 9,000 years ago, enclosing a town of around 2,000 people. This clay-covered skull was found at the ancient site.

The ancient city of Catal Huyuk in today's Turkey is around 8,000 years old, and it was occupied for many centuries.

Amongst the houses, this fresco of hunters surrounding a great red bull must have adorned a special religious place.

Where the climate was good and the land fertile, people chose to become farmers. They grew food instead of hunting for it. With more than enough to eat inside the new farming settlements, some villagers were free to learn crafts or to build homes, and the first cities of the world began to take shape. The growth of the world's first cities is called the Urban Revolution, and it was most widespread in the Nile delta and between the rivers Tigris and Euphrates around 5,000 years ago. Many thousands of people started living together in new class systems, with ruling families in charge at the top, and workers and slaves at the bottom.

The first cities usually had strong stone walls protecting the homes inside. The gates of the city were guarded by soldiers and were locked at night or if the city was under attack. Market stalls were set up at the gateways to attract buyers going through the city gates.

Safe inside the walls, the people started to develop writing, science, and astronomy – and built great temples and palaces.

The Assyrian city of **Korsabad** (742-706 BC) had temples and palaces built within its strong walls.

The great city of Jericho was one of the world's earliest cities, although many of the great ancient cities grew up in river valleys. Jericho's thick stone walls date back thousands of years to the Neolithic Age, when people began to settle and farm. Nearby water was vital to their survival.

Most urban societies divided themselves into separate classes.

Ruling families

Priests

Nobles

Important citizens

Merchants and Craftsmen

Workers and slaves

Most of the world's first great cities developed in fertile river valleys.

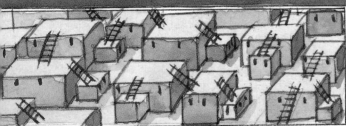

c. 6000 BC The ancient city of Catal Huyuk was built of mud-bricks. The flat-roofed houses were so close together that the only way to travel about was across the rooftops!

5000 BC Egyptian and Mesopotamian farmers use river water to irrigate their fields.

3000 BC Cities appear independently in different parts of the world, beginning in the Middle East at Ur, Uruk, Babylon and Nineveh.

Nineveh

Babylon

Uruk

Ur

Persian Gulf

ANCIENT MONUMENTS

The Sumerians and the Egyptians were the first to build great monumental buildings but many ancient civilisations followed their example. Made of brick or stone, these were buildings meant to last, and to demonstrate the power of their gods and kings.

PAGAN EUROPE

Circles and lines of standing stones were ingeniously raised on sites across western Europe, from Sweden to Malta and also in the British Isles. The stones' purpose is a mystery but their siting was the work of Stone Age people, organised into huge teams, who dragged the massive stones long distances across the landscape and set them upright.

THE ROMANS

The Romans ruled Italy from around 265 BC, and also conquered North Africa, around the Mediterranean and southern Europe and into Asia Minor. Roman public buildings were copied throughout the Empire under emperors from Augustus (31 BC) onward, and their grid-designed cities were built in stone, brick, volcanic rock (tufa, pumice and lava), terracotta and concrete. Concrete was a great invention, allowing Romans to develop arches, vaults and domes.

① **Stonehenge** grew in size over many centuries, into an impressive stone circle. The massive outer sandstone blocks weighed about 40 tonnes, and the inner blue stones were dragged 240 kilometres (150 miles) from Preselly in Wales to Salisbury Plain.

② **Hadrian's Wall** was built in about 122 AD, at the height of the Roman Empire. The Emperor Hadrian ordered the great stone wall to be built in Britannia, at the edge of his empire. Acting as a defence and as a frontier trading control, it lay between Roman-occupied land and Scotland to the north.

ANCIENT GREECE & CRETE

Ancient Crete (c. 2000-1450 BC), with its Minoan palaces and mythical Minotaur, was an early manifestation of the civilisation of Ancient Greece. Later, in around 1250 BC, on the mainland of Mycenae, the Greek civilisation built palaces and royal tombs. Around 500 BC, great city-states like Athens built magnificent temples and theatres.

③ **The Tomb of Agammemnon/the Treasury of Atreus** at Mycenae was a beehive-shaped 13-metre-high (43 feet) chamber, built underground but open to the sky, with a corridor access cut into the hillside.

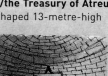

Map labels: ② GREAT BRITAIN, ① , Carnac, FRANCE, ITALY, Rome, SPAIN, GREECE, ③ CRETE, Mediterranean sea

Monumental buildings of the ancient world were built to last forever.

4700 BC Western Europeans begin to erect stone religious monuments like at Carnac in Brittany (France).

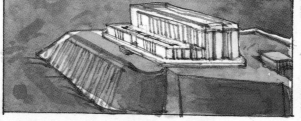

c. 3200 BC The White Temple, Uruk is built of stone, brick & tile. Protective limewash gives it its name.

3200 – 2400 BC Simple brick or stone tombs (mastabas) are first built at Memphis, Egypt's capital and centre of government in its Old Kingdom.

ASSYRIA (c. 1100–600 BC)

The borders of this empire reached from the Persian Gulf to the Mediterranean, and up to the Black Sea. The fierce Assyrians lived in northern Mesopotamia by the River Tigris, but their army defeated strong Syrian, Babylonian, Egyptian, Judean and Phoenician forces to create the largest empire of its day.

④ The ziggurat temple at Ashur

(c. 1250 BC) Between 3000–500 BC, all the great Mesopotamian city-states built brick ziggurats. The Assyrians built 3 at their capital, Ashur. The walls were very thick to compensate for the weak mud bricks, and the builders also added whitewash or patterned, coloured cones to further protect the temples.

MESOPOTAMIA

Sumerians built stepped pyramids called ziggurats in cities like Uruk, on man-made, stepped mounds. The temple stood at the top. Sargon the Great of Akkad conquered the Sumerians in c. 2800 BC.

⑤ The Pillar Temple, Uruk

(c. 3000–2500 BC) had free-standing, coloured palm tree-style pillars. The temple was decorated with coloured mud cone mosaics and could be seen from great distances. It symbolised the bridge between the gods and people.

BABYLON

Lying for 2,000 years on the banks of the River Euphrates, Babylon (c. 600 BC) was at the centre of a great empire. King Nebuchadnezzar fortified Babylon and created gardens to make it one of the most beautiful Mesopotamian cities, and a centre for trade and learning.

⑥ Tower of Babel

This 7-storey spiral ziggurat of Etemenanki was faced with blue-glazed bricks, and rose from a 90 metre (295 feet) square base.

PERSIA

The Persian Empire finally included Babylon, Anatolia, Palestine, and even parts of Egypt and India. Darius the 1st built a palace at Persepolis in a distinctive Persian style, using craftsmen from Assyria, Egypt and Greece, and Babylonian brick-makers.

⑦

Persepolis's **Hall of a Hundred Columns** (begun c. 518 BC) used glazed, coloured bricks. The painted wooded ceiling was held up by a forest of columns.

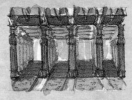

EGYPT

Menes, the first known Egyptian king, united the Upper and Lower Egyptian kingdoms in c. 3200 BC. People believed the Pharaohs were gods as well as kings and the buildings that housed their bodies symbolised their royal power in the Afterlife.

⑧ The 3 pyramids and the sphinx at Giza

(c. 2500 BC). The Great Pyramid was 146 metres (480 feet) high. The burial chamber was 70 metres (230 feet) above ground in the exact centre of the pyramid. The granite sarcophagus had been dragged into the granite-lined chamber.

They represented the power of the civilisation's gods and kings.

c. 1500–1100 BC Mycenaeans build fortifications in Greece.

c. 600 BC King Nebuchadnezzar orders the building of Babylon's Hanging Gardens.

c. 500–300 BC A great palace is begun by Darius the Great at Persepolis, the new capital of his Persian Empire.

Imhotep

Pharaoh Djoser

THE STEP PYRAMID
Saqqara, Egypt, c. 2680 BC

Imhotep's stepped pyramid was built of stone to last for 'eternity', and was much stronger than earlier mud-brick mastaba tombs.

Work masters organised many thousands of labourers into work gangs. These gangs hacked the limestone blocks out of solid rock using copper chisels and dragged the heavy blocks up ramps. Skilled craftsmen shaped the stone and made sure each layer was set perfectly level. Their tools were incredibly accurate, leaving just tiny joints to be filled with mortar.

This was the first great stone building in the world. Built at Saqqara on the banks of the River Nile, it stood a gigantic 60 metres (196 feet) high! The Pyramid's creator was Imhotep, the first architect we know of in history. It was built for Pharaoh Djoser. Deep underground, below the impressive pyramid, Imhotep planned the dead Pharaoh's real burial chamber. It was hidden to protect his mummified body and possessions he would need in the Afterlife. The ancient Egyptians did not want tomb robbers to steal what they believed belonged to their king in his eternal life after death. Like the other famous pyramids at nearby Giza, the Step Pyramid was built with astonishing accuracy. After studying the night sky, surveyors carefully aligned its site exactly to the compass points of north, south, east and west.

Giza
Saqqara
Memphis

Imhotep's pyramid was the main feature in a huge network of temples and tombs, built to house the remains and belongings of royal family members. The whole area was a place for rituals of death.

It took many years of skilful organisation to plan, find labour, then build the pyramid.

3000–2500 BC The 900-towered great wall of Uruk is built.

c. 2500 BC Using simple ropes and levers, workers drag rock-laden sledges higher and higher up ramps to complete the pyramids.

2100–1500 BC On the island of Crete, the Minoans build a famous palace at Knossos.

1250 BC The new temple at Karnak in Egypt is dedicated to the god Amun.

Iktinos and Kallikrates

THE PARTHENON
Athens, Greece, 447–38 BC

GREECE
•Athens

The architects used visual tricks on the temple. Columns that bulged outwards slightly, actually looked straight. Although they looked equally spaced, the columns were spaced unevenly and leaned inwards. Even the plinth bulged upwards to make it appear flat.

The Parthenon was just a part of the sacred site called the Akropolis. Processions approached by walking up a steep, easily-defended hill and through an entrance gate. Inside were temples and statues.

Labourers and oxen had to haul everything up to the Akropolis. Men shifted stones into place using simple ramps and cranes but gravity and metal clamps held most of the stonework together.

This impressive marble temple took just 9 years to build. Perikles, a famous statesman from Athens, commissioned it and dedicated it to the goddess Athena – the Greek goddess of wisdom. The temple was a place to meet and worship – a typical Greek temple of columns, lintels, and massive roof timbers. But the Parthenon's beautiful design and magnificent position is what makes it special. The architects worked out every proportion in tiny detail to make the finished temple appear perfect. There are 8 columns at each end of the Parthenon, and 17 along the sides. All of them rest on a 3-step plinth which provides a level base on the rocky outcrop. Originally, Athena's temple was very colourful and full of sculpture. There was a huge gold and ivory statue of Athena inside, and rich decoration on the frieze and pediments.

Today, the Parthenon is a ruin as it was used for storing gunpowder in the 18th century and an explosion blew off the roof. Many of the sculptures located in the frieze were broken up and sold to a British diplomat called Lord Elgin. They can be seen at the British Museum in London.

The Greeks devised certain styles of capitals for the temple columns, and for all other vertical shapes on the temple.

Doric capitals
The simplest of the styles, the capital (top of the column) is carved from a single stone block.

Ionic capitals
A style originating on the Ionian coast, the Ionic capital is more decorative than the Doric.

Corinthian capitals
Based on the Ionic style, the Corinthian capital also has a stylised acanthus leaf decoration.

Athens, a rich city-state, built a 'perfect' marble temple on the summit of the rocky Akropolis.

c. 600 BC In the city of Babylon, King Nebuchadnezzar builds the magnificent Ishtar Gate using blue-glazed bricks.

300 BC Dinocrates and Greek engineers build the Egyptian city of Alexandria, and a great lighthouse on the island of Pharos at the mouth of the Nile.

c. 210 BC Emperor Qin Shi Huang Ti rules a newly-unified China, and builds the 6,000 kilometre (3,730 mile) long Great Wall along China's northern boundary, to protect them from invading Huns.

THE COLOSSEUM
Rome, Italy, AD 70 – 82

Emperor Vespasian AD 9 – 79

awnings

seating levels

As commander of the Roman army, Vespasian had invaded Britain in AD 43, decades before he became the emperor. The Colosseum actually came to be named after a huge statue of the Emperor Nero, erected just outside the amphitheatre.

Roman emperors took a keen interest in architecture. Hadrian may have designed his own villa at Tivoli (AD 118 –134), with its pavilions, follies, baths and libraries, all set in beautiful gardens.

The amphitheatre showed off two brilliant Roman inventions – arches and concrete. Roman concrete arches, vaults and barrel vaults were very strong. Roman concrete was made from sand, lime or pozzolana, a type of volcanic rock, mixed with water.

The ruins of Rome's near perfect amphitheatre, the Colosseum, still stand today, 2,000 years after brilliant Roman engineers built it. It is the model for all modern stadiums. After Emperor Vespasian commissioned the famous amphitheatre, 10 years of hard work passed before its completion. Its outside wall had 3 levels of arches or arcades, decorated with Doric, Ionic and Corinthian columns.

Such a massive building had to have strong, deep foundations. Engineers made them of solid concrete, to support the amphitheatre's warren of brick-lined vaults. Arches, vaults and concrete were all Roman inventions. Gladiators, wild animals and captives were all housed under the Colosseum in a maze of rooms, pens and cages. They made their way to the arena to entertain 50,000 excited spectators. The most important of these sat at the ringside – slaves, women and foreigners were right at the top. But they all relished the violent and bloody shows and games.

Trajan's Column built about AD 112 is a 35-metre-high (115 feet) monument celebrating the Emperor's victories in the wars in Dacia (today's Romania).

Roman engineers learnt to use strong arches to span wide spaces.

c. AD 14 Roman engineers build an aqueduct at Pont du Gard, in the south of France.

AD 120 – 124 Emperor Hadrian builds a technological masterpiece in Rome – a massive concrete-domed Pantheon temple.

AD 180 Romans build a theatre at Sabratha in Libya, North Africa.

Isidoros of Miletos & Anthemios of Tralles

HAGIA SOPHIA
Istanbul, Turkey, AD 532–37

Emperor Justinian the 1st

The beautiful Hagia Sophia means *Divine Wisdom*, and was the largest Christian church built for the Roman Emperor Justinian the 1st in Constantinople (now Istanbul). It had 4 strong stone piers to support a shallow dome that was put there to cover the huge basilica below. Arches linked these corner piers, and to the east and west, smaller piers supported more small half-domes. This design allowed the cathedral's nave to be a huge, uncluttered, 70-metre-long (230 feet) oval space. Windows in the dome and in the walls lit Hagia Sophia's interior, and craftsmen decorated the inside of the dome with spectacular, colourful marbles and mosaics. For 900 years, until 1453, Hagia Sophia was the most important Christian church in the Eastern Roman Empire. But when Constantinople was conquered by the Turks, they turned Hagia Sophia into a mosque for Muslim worship and made some additions to the building.

In 1935 the building became a museum.

When the Western Roman Empire fell in the 5th century, the empire broke up into lots of local cultures, and for a long time no one wanted to build impressive, new buildings. But in the rich Byzantine Empire, the capital, Constantinople, was still successful. Its new buildings were simple but highly decorated – mixing Roman brickwork and concrete engineering with Middle Eastern-style domes. Constantinople's distinctive style lasted for a thousand years.

A basilica is a large oblong hall. The earliest known basilica was built by the Romans in 184 BC and was the basis for Christian churches throughout western Europe.

Domed 6th century churches like Hagia Sophia set the style for Christian churches in the Eastern Roman Empire. Domes over a circular space do not allow much variety in building design but domes over a square space, like Hagia Sophia's dome, became a model for later Renaissance domes like the one used for St Peter's Basilica in Rome (see page 24).

Hagia Sophia-style domes adorned churches throughout the old Eastern Roman empire.

c. AD 500 The Mayan Temple of the Great Jaguar is built at the large city of Tikal (in today's Mexico).

AD 522 A towering pagoda is built in Honan, China.

AD 547 The beautiful San Vitale church is built in Ravenna, Italy.

THE GREAT MOSQUE
Cordoba, Spain, begun AD 785

Caliph Harun al-Rashid

Mecca's Ka'ba

The Islamic religion began through the work of the prophet Mohammed (born in Mecca, AD 569). As a man, Mohammed wrote down the words of Allah (God) in the holy Koran – words his followers used to inspire Arabian tribes. In the 7th century, Muslim armies, called the Moors, set out on a campaign to convert more people to Islam in the Middle East, India and North Africa. They moved on to conquer Spain. Christianity in western Europe was under threat until Charles Martel, the king of France (AD 714–41) defeated the Islamic forces at Tours and Poitiers. The Moors remained in Spain until the 15th century.

ISLAMIC WORLD

This Great Mosque in southern Spain was the work of Syrian builders who were using North African building styles. But they allowed local brick and stone building skills to play their part. Here in Cordoba, in Spain, the architects and builders used Roman marble columns (taken from old ruins) for the main part of the mosque. The ten rows were made taller by adding an extra stilt-like column to create unusual 'horseshoe' arches, under the high sanctuary roof. All the beautiful arches and vaults were strikingly decorated. In this, the Great Mosque followed the Koran's strict Islamic rules about design and decoration. In religious places, images – of people or things – were absolutely forbidden. Instead, Islam encouraged exquisite abstract patterns from Arab writing, from nature and from geometry. The Great Mosque was also, importantly, built to a very human scale. Unlike Christian cathedrals, it was never meant to be towering and monumental.

After Mohammed's death in 632 AD, a succession of caliphs took over as civic and religious rulers. Caliph Harun al-Rashid was the leader of the Abbayid Caliphate (786-809 AD), at the time of the building of the Great Mosque at Cordoba.

SPAIN
Madrid
PORTUGAL
Cordoba

After the 8th century, work continued on Cordoba's Great Mosque from AD 961 to 966 and also AD 987 to 990. Builders added more rows of arches and columns.

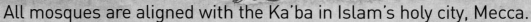
All mosques are aligned with the Ka'ba in Islam's holy city, Mecca.

AD 688 The Kubbet es-Sakhra (Dome of the Rock) is built in Jerusalem as a shrine. It has a high dome, and inside, Islamic-style decoration in mosaic, marble and glass. The outside is also richly decorated with patterned mosaic tiles.

Islamic-style geometric tiling

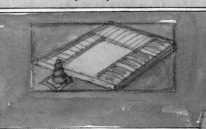
AD 848 Caliph Al-Mutawakkil designs the Great Mosque at Sammara in Iraq. It has a giant spiral minaret, a prayer hall and an enclosing wall. People can actually ride horses to the top of the minaret!

ANGKOR WAT
Cambodia, c. 12th century

Vishnu

BURMA

INDIA CAMBODIA

JAVA

Buddha

India's Buddhist religion spread east to other parts of Asia. Like the Hindu temple, a Buddhist temple was also built to look like a mountain. At the top was a bell-like tower called a stupa – the pilgrims' goal – which symbolised Eternal Truth.

Angkor Wat, originally a Hindu temple, later became a Buddhist shrine.

For a hundred years, from the 2nd to the 3rd centuries, India's culture – especially its Buddhist and Hindu religions – spread east outside its borders to Burma, Cambodia and Java. Angkor Wat's Hindu temple is one of the greatest examples of this influence. According to custom, pilgrims walked around the temple – a distance of 21 kilometres (13 miles)! The temple's high towers protect sacred shrines and symbolise India's mythological Mount Mehru – the gods' home – stretching from deep below the ground, up to the heavens.

This huge and extraordinary building, 1,550 metres long by 1,400 metres wide (4,920 feet long by 4,600 feet wide), is the largest temple complex in Cambodia's great city of Angkor. Surprisingly, it was lost for centuries in overgrown forest.

King Suryavarman the 2nd's builders constructed Angkor Wat with great skill, from massive sandstone blocks held together without mortar.

Angkor Wat was actually the King's tomb. It was meant to show off his great power and to celebrate the Hindu god, Vishnu. Surrounded by walls and an 8-metre-wide (26 feet) moat, its shape represents the Indian mythological Mount Mehru, home of the gods. Extraordinarily long colonnades stand on a series of Angkor Wat's platforms, and at the building's heart there are five sandstone lotus bud-shaped towers. They are beautifully carved and decorated, just like the temple's lower walls and roof.

corbelled arch

The Buddhist 'temple-mountain' at Borobudur in Java, c. AD 800.

Angkor Wat was one of India's greatest monumental buildings, outside its borders.

12th century The Burmese king, Kyanzitthar builds the Ananda temple at Pagan, imitating what monks had told him about India's cave-temple at Orissa. Ananda's roofed temple, on carved platform-terraces, has staircases leading 52 metres (170 feet) up to the dome-shaped stupa. Underneath, inside the temple, are 4 huge standing Buddhas.

Emperor Otto the 3rd

ROMANESQUE
c. 10th-12th centuries

Europe's educated monks designed the new Romanesque churches and cathedrals for their rich monasteries, and skilled masons and carpenters built them. The monk-architects planned these buildings carefully. They had to be simple structures – solid and well built – yet every part of the design had a real function. For instance, there were chapels for mass and ambulatories behind the high altar where pilgrims could walk. All the parts combined into one whole beautiful building that included special Romanesque elements within it – like the massive, decorated stone columns that held up semi-circular arches and ribbed vaulting in the ceiling.

The new Romanesque era began in c. AD 981 when Emperor Otto the 3rd, of Europe's Holy Roman Empire helped the Church rebuild the old Abbey Church at Cluny in Burgundy, France.

Popes wielded great power in the 11th and 12th centuries and the Church owned large estates. So kings and noblemen generously supported the rich monasteries. Western Europe had a healthy economy. Its towns and cities were growing in size and confidence, and naturally, the rival cities and countries vied to build bigger and better churches.

At a time of stable and well-organised societies in western Europe, the church – and the feudal rulers like the Norman kings – could afford to build magnificent new stone buildings and churches. Norman conquests took their new Romanesque building style from France to England (after 1066), then to Sicily and Italy (1071) and even to Rome (1084).

PISA CATHEDRAL (1063)
The famous Romanesque cathedral at Pisa in Italy sits amongst later, famous buildings – the **Baptistry** (1153–1265) and the **Leaning Tower** (1174–1271). During the 12th and 13th centuries, Pisa was a wealthy place, and wanted beautiful architecture to show off to its rival cities. The cathedral is a simple basilica shape, but decorated outside with dazzling arcades and coloured marble. Inside, columns divide the nave and the cathedral's aisles. But one new element, the transept, crossed the nave, and turned the church plan into the sacred shape of a cross – an idea used by all the later medieval cathedrals.

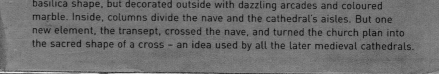

Monks designed ancient Roman-style round arches for their heavy and solid Romanesque cathedrals.

1068 Caen's St-Etienne is begun in France in a Norman style. Inside the church, the nave is pierced with columns and arches.

1090 The impressive curtain wall of Rochester Castle is begun for the local bishop. The keep is built later, around 1127, for the Archbishop of Canterbury.

1093 Builders start work on Durham Cathedral, creating some of the earliest, decorative rib-vaulting in England.

GOTHIC
c. 12th-14th centuries

Trade was booming in the 13th century. Europe and the Church remained prosperous. When every thriving town demanded its own cathedral, master-craftsmen - helped by craft-guilds - took over from monks as the new church architects. Similarly, the heavy Romanesque style gave way to a lighter Gothic style. This Gothic style first appeared near Paris in 1122, when the new Abbot, Suger, ordered changes to the Abbey of St Denis. When finished, it featured all the new, delicate, Gothic elements – rib vaults, pointed arches and flying buttresses. The thin columns, high roof and walls and the many huge windows gave Gothic cathedrals a feeling of space and light.

The old feudal class systems were beginning to break down. Poor serfs – once tied to their Lord's land - began finding work in towns, learning new skills, and going up in the world. A new urban middle class of rich merchants were now as powerful as the Church and old barons. Town merchants controlled their own trade and taxes, as well as artists and the guilds (unions) of craftsmen, traders and builders. It was the guilds who now supplied skilled men (designers, masons, carpenters, carvers, glaziers and even painters) for important new building projects.

The first Gothic cathedral mason-builders were practical, inventive builders and good mathematicians. Their skills were in such demand that they travelled all across Europe for work. By the 14th century, they were held in great respect, raising their status. Some even married into the nobility!

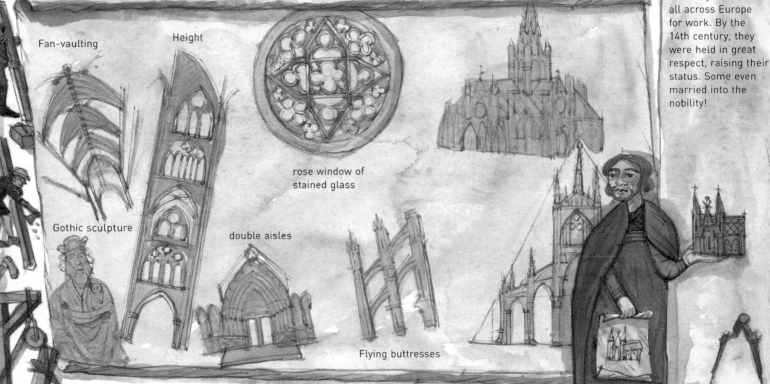

Fan-vaulting

Height

rose window of stained glass

Gothic sculpture

double aisles

Flying buttresses

Master masons built towering yet delicate Gothic cathedrals using pointed arches and buttressing.

1130s–1140s The Abbey Church of St Denis, near Paris, has Europe's first example of the light, airy Gothic style.

Late 12th century Canterbury Cathedral has fine stained glass windows including one of St Thomas Becket, murdered there in 1170.

1220 Long and tall Salisbury Cathedral is built quickly (1220–60), and has a spacious nave and beautiful stonework.

Robert de Luzarches

AMIENS CATHEDRAL
Amiens, France, 1220–88

Elaborate sculptures called gargoyles were used under gutters to project water away from the walls.

The biggest Gothic cathedral in the whole of Europe was at Amiens in France. In 1220 Bishop Evrard de Fouilloy commissioned Robert de Luzarches, a master mason, to build it. De Luzarches' cathedral was clearly different from the old, heavy Romanesque look. Using stone from quarries near Amiens, he created a towering church with beautiful stained glass windows that filled it with colour and light. Unlike Romanesque churches, his Gothic cathedral had walls that were thin and high — and pierced by huge windows. This was possible because masons had invented buttresses to support the huge weight of the walls from the outside.

De Luzarches showed off his other skills too. He carved the window sculptures including the larger than life-size apostles and prophets, and 'The Last Judgement' scenes over the central entrance door. In 1288, another mason completed the last job at Amiens — an intricate labyrinth design in the nave floor.

In Gothic times, society had many levels. At the top were royalty and powerful clergy. Below them were the landowners, merchants and craftsmen. At the bottom were the peasants. Anyone with money invested in building. The Church built cathedrals, lords built castles and manors, merchants and guildsmen built towns and the

peasants built their own humble cottages.

Every prosperous French town, like Amiens, wanted a soaring Gothic cathedral of its own.

12th century Peasants build humble cottages, called hovels, to live in.

12th century The Jew's House in Lincoln is first stone house known to have been built in England.

1165–67 Alnoth, Henry the 2nd's ingeniator (designer) builds Orford Castle in Suffolk, England.

1163–1250 Master masons direct the building of Notre Dame Cathedral in Paris.

PALAZZO VECCHIO

Florence, Italy, 1298–1322

Arnolfo di Cambio

ITALY

Venice
Florence
Siena
Rome

Towers were built in some Italian towns in medieval times to protect the town against theft and to display the power of a ruling family or town council.

Many people think that the Palazzo Vecchio – one of Italy's many magnificent medieval town halls – was built by the sculptor and architect Arnolfo di Cambio. The Palazzo was constructed very quickly between 1299 and 1310 – just three years after he had begun another of Florence's famous buildings – the Duomo, or Cathedral.

Florence's colossal Palazzo Vecchio (meaning 'Old Palace') was built as a town hall in Piazza della Signoria at the heart of the city's government area. The bell in the palace's 95-metre-high (312 feet) tower often summoned people to public meetings, or warned them of approaching danger. Most of the 13th-century Palazzo was finished within 12 years, though the bell tower was completed later. In the 15th and 16th centuries, a new ruling family called the Medicis, added lavish decorations inside the palazzo, including beautiful statues and frescoes.

Many Italian towns, or their rulers, built palaces in the 12th and 13th centuries. They were usually strong stone buildings, about 5-storeys high like the Palazzo Vecchio, built to resist enemies and to impress people. To be safe from attackers, a palazzo's lower windows were smaller than those above. There were also machicolations, battlements and watchtowers, to add an even greater impression of strength.

belfry

tower

battlements

Each storey is about 10 metres high (33 feet).

Powerful groups fought to control many of Italy's wealthy cities in the 13th century. Florence had two factions. The Guelphs wanted the Pope to rule, but the Ghibellines supported Germany's Holy Roman Emperor, who had his eye on Italy. The Guelphs won in 1289, but they argued about whether they should rule themselves or let the Pope rule them from Vatican City. It wasn't until the 15th century that the Medicis, a rich banking family, took control. Florence prospered and attracted famous artists like Brunelleschi and Fra Angelico.

Rich and powerful Italian city-states, like Florence, dominated Europe in the 13th century.

1201 The Cloth Hall for Flemish wool merchants is begun in Ypres, Belgium.

1238–1358 The Moors in Spain build The Alhambra, a great Islamic city-palace in Granada, Spain.

1288 The beautiful Palazzo Pubblico is begun in Siena, bearing the highest bell tower in Italy at 102 metres (335 feet).

1309–1424 The Doge's Palace in Venice is built by Giovanni and Bartolomeo Buon for the city's powerful ruler.

THE RENAISSANCE IN ITALY
14th–16th centuries

In Renaissance times, Italy's great cities became extraordinary centres of learning and new ideas. It was not just clergymen who were searching for understanding about how the world worked. Now brilliant and inventive people outside religion were becoming involved. These talented people studied in Florence and Rome and today are called Renaissance men.

Within this dazzling group, painters were studying perspective and geometry, sculptors experimented with anatomy and musicians and architects used mathematics.

Leon Battista Alberti wrote an important book called *De Re Aedificatoria*, in 1452, and set out the mathematics behind classical architecture. Alberti's ideas were eagerly received and classical building styles were reborn in Renaissance architecture.

Filippo Brunelleschi (1377–1446) was a goldsmith and sculptor turned architect. Brunelleschi visited Rome to study its rich classical architectural history. This helped him to design buildings such as the dome of Florence's cathedral.

Library of San Marco, 1536

VENICE

Santa Maria dei Miracoli 1481–89

Il Redentore, 1577

Villa Rotonda, 1552

VICENZA

MANTUA

Sant'Andrea, 1472

BOLOGNA

Santa Maria Novella, 1456

FLORENCE

Florence Cathedral, 1436

PISA

GENOA

Venice
Though most new classical-style Renaissance architecture came to Venice after it had arrived in Rome, the first buildings were seen as early as 1460. Venice always had its own unique style, influenced by its Eastern trading links.

Florence
Under the leadership of the powerful Medici family, Florence became a peaceful and rich city. Bankers and merchants could afford to pay for beautiful paintings, and build churches, palaces and other buildings in the new Renaissance style.

Michelangelo (1475–1564) was a painter and sculptor, not an architect. Because of this, some of his designs broke strict rules about how architecture was supposed to look.

Donato Bramante (1444–1514) designed buildings in Milan before becoming one of Rome's best architects. Tempietto di San Pietro in Rome was his masterpiece, built at the spot where St Peter was martyred.

Renaissance architects were often men of many talents.

1487 Leonardo da Vinci's 'Vitruvian Man' shows the body's perfect proportions.

15th century The Renaissance view of an ideal City shows a logically planned urban area with radial, grid and star designs, wide streets and fortifications.

1568 Vignola's and della Porta's Il Gesu church in Rome will influence church design.

Leon Battista Alberti (1404–72) wrote about Rome's classical buildings. He agreed with the architectural ideas of Vitruvius, the Roman writer, and used them in churches like Florence's Santa Maria Novella, and Sant'Andrea in Mantua.

Jacopo Sansovino (1486–1570) was a sculptor from Florence. In 1536 Sansovino built the huge and highly decorated Library of San Marco, built to hold old Greek and Roman manuscripts.

Pietro Lombardo (1435–1515) built the highly patterned marble, Santa Maria dei Miracoli. The church has a simple rectangular shape, with a timber barrel-vault inside, and a dome above.

Andrea Palladio (1508–80) was a mason who studied Classical ideas, and used them in his very imaginative and original country villas around Vicenza including the Villa Rotonda (see page 25).

Renaissance ideas were not confined to science and art but to exploration as well. Henry the Navigator of Portugal paid for sea voyages round West Africa, and the route was extended to the Cape of Good Hope and eastward to India. In 1492 Columbus sailed west to the New World.

St Peter's Basilica, 1506 onwards

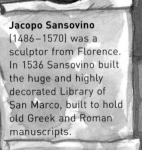

Villa Farnesina, 1509–11

Palazzo Farnese, 1515

Rome
In the 14th and 15th centuries Rome was an immensely wealthy city. The Church used its money to show off its power, just as ancient Rome's emperors had done. Classical ideas and buildings still symbolised great imperial power, and the Church wanted to copy and revive those Classical times.

● ROME

Philibert de l'Orme (1515–70) visited Italy in 1533, and liked the Classical architecture of Ancient Rome. He used Vitruvius's ideas on geometry in his own work, which often featured steep roofs, and plain lower storeys.

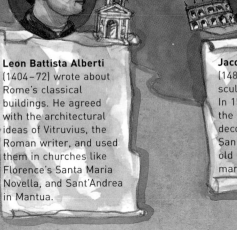

Antonio da Sangallo was Bramante's pupil, and the designer of Rome's Palazzo Farnese (1515). This impressive palace was three storeys high. Builders stole stone from the Colosseum for some of its windows!

Baldassare Peruzzi (1481–1536), a painter and architect from Siena, arrived in Rome in 1503. He worked on St Peter's Basilica before going on to design the Villa Farnesina.

They could be artists, poets or playwrights – even soldiers or   military engineers.

1475 Fioravanti and Novi build the Cathedral of the Dormiton inside Moscow's Kremlin.

1508 The beautiful church of Santa Maria della Consolazione is built at Todi in Italy.

1552-60 Giovanni Battista Quadro designs and builds Poznan's Town Hall in Poland.

1556-87 William Cecil probably designs and builds his own house at Burghley in England.

ST PETER'S BASILICA
Rome, Italy, 1506 – 1626

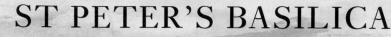

The original design for the dome

Michelangelo was a famous sculptor and artist before he took on the unpaid work of completing St Peter's. His famous sculptures include *David* in Florence, and the *Pietà* – which is inside St Peter's itself.

Nine architects worked on St Peter's! It ended up rather oversized and over-decorated. The high nave even gets in the way of views of the dome, which is best seen from the roof.

When Emperor Constantine's ancient 4th century basilica to St Peter in Rome began to crumble, the ambitious Pope Julius the 2nd commissioned a new church to replace it. It was a huge project. The experienced architect Donato Bramante won the competition with a magnificently grand design, a beautifully decorated Greek-cross church topped with a shallow central dome. He began work in 1506. The artist Raphael joined the project in 1513 and revised the design. The two architects argued but finally the brilliant Michelangelo Buonarroti took on the work in 1546. He changed Bramante's dome into a much higher one – 140 metres (460 feet) to its top – and made sure it was supported by 4 huge piers. It was held together on the inside with chains. Michelangelo worked on St Peter's until his death in 1564 but his models of the dome and cupola enabled the inside of the dome to be completed. The building was finished in 1626. In 1667, the piazza of St Peter's was built by Gian Lorenzo Bernini (see page 32). Despite all the quarrels, St Peter's is now thought of as one of the world's great Renaissance buildings.

As St Peter's first architect, Bramante drew on his earlier experience of building domes, particularly his tiny Tempietto San Pietro which was completed in 1510.

Michelangelo's magnificent St Peter's Basilica honours the Pope's patron saint.

1509 Baldassare Peruzzi begins the luxurious suburban Villa Farnesina on the banks of Rome's River Tiber.

1546 In Rome, Michelangelo takes over from Antonio da Sangallo to complete the Palazzo Farnese.

1538 – 42 The Villa Godi, one of Andrea Palladio's many rural villas, is completed in Lonedo, Italy.

VILLA ROTONDA

Vicenza, Italy, c.1552–70

Andrea Palladio (1508–80)

After studying the Classical ruins in Rome, Palladio wrote about what the ancient architects had done. Europe's new printing industry ensured that these books could be read in many countries.

San Giorgio Maggiore

Palladio also designed churches. His most famous churches, San Giorgio Maggiore (1565) and Il Redentore (1576–77), were built in Venice. They were also symmetrical. Palladio liked to use pure white stone. He thought it would be pleasing to God.

Il Redentore

Palazzo Chiericati (1550)

Palladio believed rooms and buildings should have pleasing proportions. His buildings – always symmetrical – looked simple outside, because they were made of simple shapes.

Andrea Palladio was one of the most important men in architectural history. His books, which were read throughout Europe, earned him this grand reputation and spread his architectural ideas around the world. Palladio himself had studied ancient Classical architecture in Rome and had developed theories that he and other architects put into practice. The Villa Rotonda was one of many Palladian villas. They were mostly working country homes on rich farms in the fertile Veneto area, near Venice. Palladio liked to use Roman temple façades for the entrances. But the Villa Rotonda, built on top of a hill, was far more imposing. Designed for a retired clergyman as a place where he could entertain his friends, the Rotonda was special for its lavish inside decoration and extraordinary symmetry. Outside, all four façades were identical – they resembled ancient temple façades and overlooked beautiful countryside.

Teatro Olimpico

Just before he died, Palladio designed this famous theatre. It was completed after his death in 1585.

Palladio's famous book helped him become one of Europe's most important architects.

1546 Lescot designs the Louvre Palace in Paris.

1553 Veronese completes his painting on a ceiling in the Doge's Palace, Venice.

1561 Cornelius Floris begins his ornate Town Hall in Antwerp.

1563 De Herrera begins the Escorial Palace in Madrid, for King Philip the 2nd of Spain.

Postnik & Barma

ST BASIL'S CATHEDRAL
Moscow, Russia, 1555–60

A lot of the decoration – like the colourfully tiled domes – were added in the 17th century, long after Tsar Ivan had died. Craftsmen painted the cathedral's exterior, and its iron-clad domes were replaced with the wonderfully coloured tiles we see today.

In 1550, to celebrate a Russian victory over the country's Tartar rulers, Tsar Ivan the 4th (the Terrible) ordered architects Barma and Postnik to build a magnificent cathedral in Red Square, Moscow. The result of their work was St Basil's, a traditional 'tent and tower' church with its central tower-topped church surrounded by eight smaller ones. The extraordinary building was painted white originally. It was a mixture of two Russian traditional styles – decorated brickwork and timber. St Basil's onion domes make the building particularly distinctive. It is said that Russian domes had to be that shape to let the heavy snow slide off!

Barma and Postnik were working in Renaissance times, so they also incorporated Italian style and craftsmanship, imported into Russia alongside traded goods from Venice.

Ivan the Terrible (1530–84)

Known to inspire 'awe' rather than terror, Tsar Ivan made sure that Russia was ruled strongly from the centre in Moscow. Like Henry the 8th of England, he had six wives. He could be very cruel. Ther are stories that he gouged out the eye of one architect who worked on St Basil's.

Moscow

RUSSIA

Black Sea

Shallow islamic-style domes found their way from Constantinople to Russia's Christian churches.

1505 The Bell Tower of Ivan the Terrible is begun in the Kremlin, Moscow.

1547–52 Philibert de L'Orme designs the Chateau of Anet, including its elegant chapel.

1549 Andrea Palladio designs a new façade for the town hall in his home-town of Vicenza.

1550–56 Suleiman's mosque is quickly completed in Constantinople.

Peter Street

William Shakespeare
(1564–1616)

THE GLOBE
London, England, 1599

The Globe has an amazing story. When their new lease was refused, Richard Burbage, leader of the Lord Chamberlain's Men, and builder Peter Street, demolished their old theatre (The Theatre). In the dead of night on 28th December 1598, they dismantled the theatre, carried the timbers across the Thames, and used the wood to build the new Globe at Southwark.

Master carpenter Peter Street built The Globe theatre in 1599, in the style of animal-baiting amphitheatres already seen in London. Described as a 'wooden O', it had a complicated twenty-sided oak timber frame, which rested on a low brick wall. The frame was filled with oak staves, laths and plaster, and coated with lime-wash. When the whole building was finished, it stretched 30 metres (100 feet) across.

The Globe's audience either sat in the three-tiered gallery under a thatched roof or stood in the open arena close to the raised stage. The ground was covered with hazelnut shells, ash, cinders and silt, and was strewn with rubbish when the play was finished.

The stage area and tiring house were highly decorated. Italian artists painted columns and balcony balustrades to look like marble, and more theatre magic was created by trapdoors in the heavens and on the stage. Actors made miraculous entrances through these!

William Shakespeare was an actor and playwright with the Lord Chamberlain's Men at The Globe. It was the best and richest company at that time and was rivalled only by The Lord Admiral's Men who played at The Rose theatre.

Playhouses and venues for animal-baiting were very popular in Elizabethan London. But the Lord Mayor frowned on both because of the crowds, chaos and disease that went with them. Most companies built their theatres outside the city walls, beyond his reach.

The Globe followed the traditional English timber-framed building style.

1520 King Henry the 8th takes over Cardinal Wolsey's palace at Hampton Court in England.

1538–58 Nonsuch Palace is built for Henry the 8th by Italian, Dutch and English craftsmen.

17th century View of the River Thames and the Globe at Southwark.

1619 Inigo Jones's Renaissance Banqueting Hall is built at Whitehall for royal masquerades.

1650s Craftsmen build Little Moreton Hall, which has an elaborate timber frame.

TEMPLE MAYOR

Mexico City, Mexico, c. 1500s

Tlaloc

Tlaloc was the Aztec god of rain and farming. Children were often sacrificed to him and their bodies were buried in the temple's foundations.

Like their Egyptian counterparts, the Aztecs were skilled astronomers, aligning their temples according to the movements of the stars, planets, sun and moon. They had many grisly forms of human sacrifice which priests performed daily at the temples, because they believed blood had to spilt before their gods would make the sun rise. Priests cut out a victim's beating heart then flung it down the temple steps, which ran with the victim's blood.

For centuries, people in Central America (called Mesoamerica) built impressive cities, temples and other great buildings. The Aztecs began building their own massive pyramid-style temple in the 1500s in Tenochtitlan, today's Mexico City. Years before, in 1325, the gods had sent them a sign – an eagle on a prickly pear plant. The Aztecs knew at once where their city should be, and the temple became its most sacred site – a place of blood and sacrifice.

From eye-witness drawings, we know what windowless Aztec temples looked like, and how they were built or rebuilt. An Aztec temple could be enlarged and the new temple was built over the top of the old one. Building was hard work. The Aztecs had no wheeled transport or lifting machinery. Using just wooden wedges, quarrymen hacked 40-ton slabs from the rockface. Later, on the temple site, labourers manoeuvred each stone into place where it could be plastered or polished to a shiny finish.

When the Spanish invaded in 1519, their leader Hernán Cortés was amazed at the great pyramid-temples and plazas (squares) he saw in Tenochtitlan and Teotihuacán, an earlier pre-Aztec city in today's Mexico. But through battle and disease, the European invasion destroyed Central America's great cultures – including many temples, the symbols of their power and strength.

Many victims were captured in battles with the Aztecs.

The Aztecs of Mexico built huge temples where they sacrificed captives to their gods.

1200 BC Olmec Indians near the Gulf of Mexico carve huge sculptures and build temples.

AD 300–600 People in Mexico build the city-state of Teotihuacán, its pyramids and 23 temples.

AD 300–600 Tikal Mayans from the jungles of Central America (today's Guatemala) build temples for sacrifices and worship.

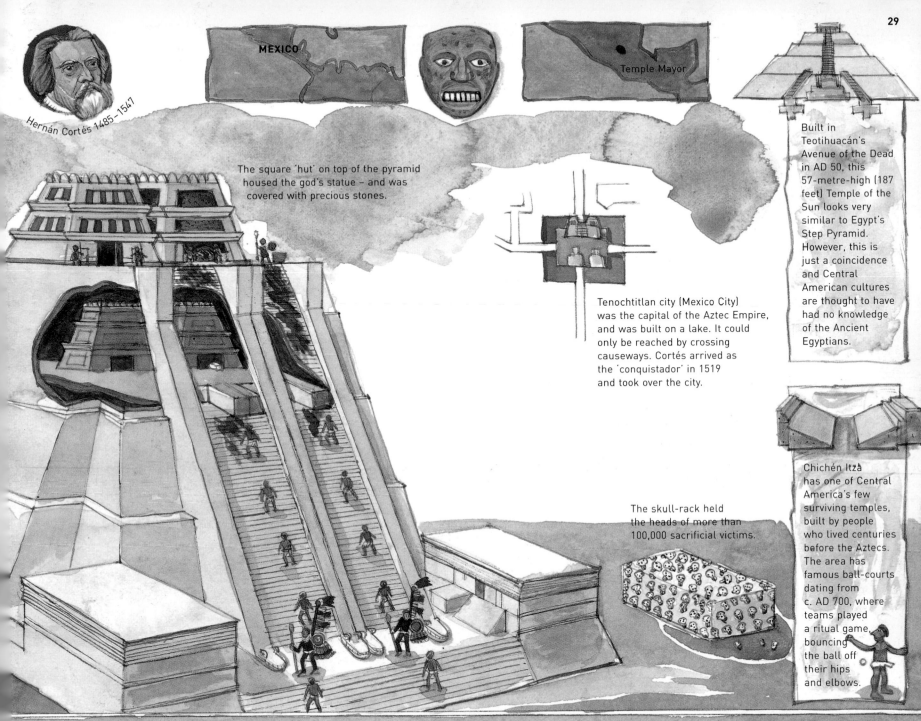

Hernán Cortés 1485–1547

MEXICO

Temple Mayor

The square 'hut' on top of the pyramid housed the god's statue – and was covered with precious stones.

Built in Teotihuacán's Avenue of the Dead in AD 50, this 57-metre-high (187 feet) Temple of the Sun looks very similar to Egypt's Step Pyramid. However, this is just a coincidence and Central American cultures are thought to have had no knowledge of the Ancient Egyptians.

Tenochtitlan city (Mexico City) was the capital of the Aztec Empire, and was built on a lake. It could only be reached by crossing causeways. Cortés arrived as the 'conquistador' in 1519 and took over the city.

The skull-rack held the heads of more than 100,000 sacrificial victims.

Chichén Itzà has one of Central America's few surviving temples, built by people who lived centuries before the Aztecs. The area has famous ball-courts dating from c. AD 700, where teams played a ritual game, bouncing the ball off their hips and elbows.

Mexico was the home of many important temple-building cultures.

AD 900–980 Invading Toltec warriors take over the Mayan centres like Chichén Itzà in today's northern Mexico.

c. 1300 The Aztecs settle in Tenochtitlan, and grow in power.

1500 Using brilliant stonework, Inca people complete Sacsahuamán, a stone fortress to defend their capital, Cuzco (in today's Peru).

BAROQUE & ROCOCO

16th century · 17th century

Gianlorenzo Bernini (1598–1680)

Francesco Borromini (1599–1667)

Antonio Vivaldi (1678–1741)

Baroque
(barocco) was a jeweller's term – meaning a rough pearl or an uncut or deformed stone. In architecture it meant a style where strict Classical rules were sometimes ignored so that the new Baroque buildings could be unusually shaped or even curved.

Many Italian cities were very rich in the 17th century. They benefited from good, strong trade - and from the wealth of the Catholic Church. Places like Rome and Florence continued to build themselves new churches and palaces (palazzi) – but now they were in the high-spirited, swirling Baroque style that the architects Giovanni Bernini and Francesco Borromini had made popular. It was a style that was part geometry and part theatre.

Bernini liked to design his buildings in a very theatrical way, using false perspectives and clever lighting. He was a sculptor who also wrote operas and plays. Bernini would happily break strict Classical and Renaissance architectural rules if he thought it made an urban space or a building more beautiful.

Borromini was a mason and a pupil of Bernini. His work was much more complicated than Bernini's – and it used even more curved, swirling shapes.

In common with the dramatic nature of Baroque architecture, Baroque composers brought new styles of music to cities like Venice. Antonio Vivaldi and Claudio Monteverdi (1567–1643) created wonderful instrumental and operatic music. The music of both composers is still played today.

San Carlo alle Quattro Fontane, Rome (1634-82)
Francesco Borromini (1599-1677)
This small, but strange and dramatic church, has an elliptical dome, and a curved façade.

Architects broke Classical rules in their curvy, highly decorated buildings.

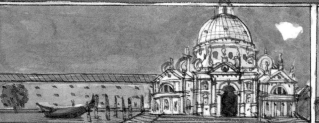

1631 Baldassare Longhena designs Venice's Santa Maria della Salute at the entrance of the Grand Canal, giving thanks to the Virgin Mary for saving Venice from the plague.

1642 Francois Mansart (1598-1666) designs the symmetrical Chateau des Maisons, balancing horizontal and vertical elements.

1667 Guarino Guarini (1624-1683) designs a complicated geometrical dome for one of Turin Cathedral's chapels that housed the Turin Shroud.

The word 'Rococo' came from the French word 'rocaille' – a type of seashell or scallop decoration. Rococo was a rich, ornamental style that was especially popular in France. The style took on the flowing lines of the rocailles shells. It fashioned elegant icing-like scrolls and swirls in gilded plasterwork which was used to decorate mirrors, walls and ceilings.

Rococo was not only used in private Paris houses like Boffrand's Hotel de Soubise (1706), but could also be found in opulent new royal apartments, like those at the Palace of Versailles (see page 33). The French white and gold Rococo colour scheme with its shell, vine and plant shapes, may have been originally inspired by Ancient Roman grottoes.

In time, Germany (especially in Bavaria), Austria and Bohemia (now the Czech Republic & Slovakia) copied the creamy colours and plasterwork scrolls when they lavishly decorated churches in the Rococo style. One fine example of this is Fischer's Abbey Church at Ottobeuren in Germany (1744-67). In these countries, the Baroque style was even more complicated and decorative. Poppelmann's fantastical Zwinger Palace (1709) at Dresden and Von Erlach's Karlskirche (see right) in Vienna, were typical.

Karlskirche, Vienna (begun 1716)
Johann Bernhard Fischer von Erlach (1656–1723)
The two columns in front of this building resemble Trajan's Column (see page 14).

Rococo was even more   fantastical than Baroque decoration.

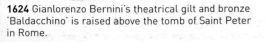

1624 Gianlorenzo Bernini's theatrical gilt and bronze 'Baldacchino' is raised above the tomb of Saint Peter in Rome.

1648 Bernini designs the *Moro* and the central *Fiumi* (pictured), two of the three fountains in Rome's Piazza Navona.

ST PETER'S PIAZZA
Rome, Italy, from 1667

Gianlorenzo Bernini (1598–1680)

Pope Alexander the 7th

In the Reformation of the 16th century, parts of the Roman Catholic Church broke away from Rome. These rebel Protestants were strongly against some Catholic rules and practices. The Catholic Church fought back in a Counter-Reformation. One way of doing this was to construct impressive new buildings in Rome.

Sant' Andrea al Quirinale y Gianlorenzo Bernini

Late in his career, Bernini, the son of a Florence sculptor, created one more grand design, the huge piazza of St Peter's in Rome. The Pope wanted to show that Rome was the powerful centre of Europe's revitalised Catholic Church, and he commissioned the new building. Bernini's answer was a design for a piazza in front of St Peter's. His plan was to surround the vast oval space with two sweeping colonnades.

Bernini loved dramatic design, and his piazza took centre stage in a plan to improve Rome's jumbled city centre. First, he hid buildings already in place, like papal offices, a palace and a library. Then he built the curving colonnade, a forest of 300 giant Doric columns, 4 rows deep, to direct pilgrims' eyes towards St Peter's itself. Bernini said that his classical columns symbolised the 'motherly arms of the church'.

The great oval of the piazza itself, became the stage for holy spectacles and the widest part of the oval piazza is 200 metres across (650 feet). He put 3 monuments there: 2 fountains, and an Egyptian obelisk that was once a turning-post for chariot races at the ancient Circus of Nero!

Colonnade of Doric columns

Bernini's Cornaro Chapel, built in Santa Maria della Vittoria in 1646.

Bernini was a man of many talents. His skills as a playwright and stage designer helped make his Classical-Baroque buildings so dramatic. Bernini's church architecture had sweeping curves, pediments and even wings like stage scenery

Inside his buildings Bernini mixed sculpture, painting and architecture in one grand theatrical design.

1658–70 Bernini builds the showy and dramatic Sant' Andrea al Quirinale church in Rome.

1662–1679 Carlo Rainaldi's Piazza del Popolo makes a further improvement to Rome's cityscape with the twin churches of Santa Maria dei Monte Santo and Santa Maria dei Miracoli.

1663 Bernini adds the Scala Regia to his Vatican designs in Rome.

THE PALACE OF VERSAILLES

Paris, France, mostly 1661–1756

André Le Notre (1613–1700)

Jules Hardouin-Mansart (1646–1708)

Louis Le Vau (1612–70)

Louis the 14th (1638–1715)

Louis the 14th's nickname, the *Sun King*, came from his admiration of the Roman Sun god, Apollo. Louis was a very good dancer, and would sometimes appear in dances dressed as Apollo. At his palace Louis enjoyed fine paintings and watched many popular plays of the time.

Louis the 14th, the Sun King, was the absolute monarch of France for an amazing 72 years, when the country's manners and culture were the envy of Europe. He controlled French tax-collecting and spending, so it was easy to order a new palace. He chose Versailles, just outside Paris. Having all his court and government under one roof meant he was able control them more easily.

The Sun King's Palace extended his father's earlier, simple Versailles estate buildings, which included a hunting lodge. The new Versailles had to be dazzling enough to symbolise Louis the 14th's absolute power — so it was huge.

Le Notre designed Versailles' gardens, which were huge and spectacular. His formal design was laid out just like a city. To entertain visitors, he put in avenues and vistas. The garden also had canal-side drives for riders and carriages, leading away to a forest. By clearing woodland, Le Notre created space for paths, terraces, pools and statues.

Le Vau and Hardouin-Mansart designed it as a central block with two wings arranged around a noble courtyard. The gardens were 400 metres (1,300 feet) long.

It was in the gardens where Louis chose to hold his three-day banquets. Inside the palace, Mansart's spectacular 70-metre-long (230 feet) Galerie des Glaces – panelled with glittering Rococo-style mirrors – was the most impressive room in a palace of luxurious apartments.

Galerie des Glaces

Louis the 14th's spectacular palace at Versailles reflected his absolute power.

1648 Van Campen designs Amsterdam's Palladian-style stone Town Hall (later the royal palace).

1649–91 On a steep mountain slope in Lhasa, Tibet, the Chinese build the 9-storey Potala Palace for the Dalai Lama.

1663 Barelli and Zuccali build their Theatine church in Munich in an Italian-baroque style.

1679 Frenchman J.B. Mathey designs Prague's Baroque-style Troja Palace.

Christopher Wren (1632–1723)

ST PAUL'S CATHEDRAL
London, England, 1675–1710

Wren had rebuilt around fifty of London's churches by the mid-1680s, every one on its tiny original site. His style was less theatrical than European Catholic churches, but the churches were nevertheless beautiful – like perfect gems. Each had a square floor plan, an upper gallery of seating – and a large pulpit that was easily seen by the entire congregation. Outside, a distinctive tall tower marked each church's location on London's crowded streets.

In his long and brilliant career, Wren designed some of England's finest buildings. It was London's terrible Great Fire in 1666 that gave him his greatest opportunity. After the destruction, King Charles the 2nd asked the young architect to rebuild London's parish churches including the great St Paul's, London's old Gothic cathedral. To please the city's religious leaders, Wren had to make a new, plain Protestant style for the churches – nothing ornate and Catholic. For St Paul's, he planned something bolder. Remembering domed churches he had seen in France, he made a magnificent wooden Great Model of the new cathedral. It had a Greek-cross shape, a dome, and one long western 'arm'. But Church leaders said it looked too Roman. Instead, they liked another of Wren's designs – a traditional Latin-cross shape, with a spire and a plain interior. Cleverly, Wren made many changes along the way. St Paul's ended up with a semicircular dome – held up by 8 strong piers, which is nearly as big as St Peter's in Rome. Wren finished building in 1710, by which time he was an old man.

Bernini's Louvre design

Wren wasn't a trained architect, but he did read Vitruvius's and Palladio's books on architecture. When he visited France, he met the famous architects Mansart and Bernini, and he saw Versailles Palace and the Louvre. Back home in England, he was a great admirer of Inigo Jones's London buildings.

part of Versailles design

Wren was a mathematician and astronomer so he understood a building's structure and space.

1699–1712 Hawksmoor and Vanbrugh design and build the Baroque-style Castle Howard in Yorkshire, a huge, winged and domed country house.

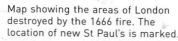
Map showing the areas of London destroyed by the 1666 fire. The location of new St Paul's is marked.

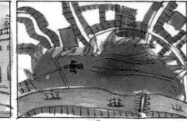
1714–29 Hawksmoor builds Christ Church, Spitalfields, influenced strongly by Italy's famous architect, Andrea Palladio.

TAJ MAHAL
Agra, India, 1630–53

Shah Jahan

Mumtaj Mahal

minaret

cupola

Great Mosque

The Mughals came from Persia (today's Iran). In 1526 they invaded India and ruled until 1761. The Mughals left behind beautiful art and harmonious architecture, like the Great Mosque (1644) and the Pearl Mosque (1662), both in Delhi.

Pearl Mosque

Delhi
Agra

INDIA

In the Islamic religion, Paradise is a garden with water. This type of garden can be found at the Taj Mahal.

During his 1628–58 reign, the great Mughal Emperor Shah Jahan built many beautiful buildings. Perhaps the most famous and most beautiful was the Taj Mahal at Agra, which he built as a tomb for his beloved Queen, Mumtaj Mahal. Despite its size, the Taj Mahal's white marble dome, cupolas and minarets seem to float above the formal canal and walled gardens in the bright Indian light. Inside, at its centre, the royal tombs are placed under the high 61-metre-high (200 feet) dome, behind screens of marble and jewels.

The Taj Mahal shows many signs of Persian and Islamic workmanship. First there are the gardens and minarets. Craftsmen have also carved Islamic-style inlaid patterns and Koranic inscriptions in the stonework, and the dome style must have travelled from Persia. People believe that the Taj Mahal is a perfect building, because it is so beautifully proportioned, like the Parthenon in Greece.

Persian Mughal invaders bring beautiful Islamic architecture to India.

1630-1680 The High Baroque style of building is popular in Italy.

1639 Shah Jahan builds the amazing Red Fort in Delhi.

1644 Cornaro Chapel in Rome's Santa Maria della Vittoria contains Bernini's sculpture of St Theresa.

THE ENLIGHTENMENT

1720s – 1820s

The 18th century saw many changes in Europe and in the USA. People began to believe that humans could conquer all challenges, simply with the power of Thought – and they called it the Age of Reason or the Enlightenment. Architects took a Grand Tour to Italy and Greece with their rich clients, taking inspiration from the distant past. On their return, their buildings took on these classical styles.

The Grand Tour was the thing to do, from the mid-18th century. Rich tourists – cultured men as well as artists and architects – journeyed through Italy and Greece, studying ancient Classical ruins and temples as they went.

PALLADIANISM

Ancient Rome was the model for the new style named after Italian architect Andrea Palladio (1508–1580). He had built Classical-style villas outside Venice, Italy. 200 years later European architects designed their own elegant Classical-style buildings.

NEO-CLASSICAL

In an era when human reason was highly prized, European and American architects chose the solemn grandeur of Ancient Greek and Roman building styles to convey the power of their own great nations.

Palladian-style town squares, and crescents became fashionable in 18th century Britain (in elegant places like Bath, London and Edinburgh), in Dublin in Ireland – and in Boston, USA. John Wood and his son designed the famous **Royal Circus and Royal Crescent in Bath**. The style even worked for the humblest townhouse.

Lord Burlington's **Chiswick House** (1723–29) looked like Palladio's beautiful Villa Rotonda at Vicenza (see page 25).

Jacques-Germain Soufflot's **Panthéon** (1756–90) in Paris was a pure but light sort of Greek architecture. He used a simple structure that had a plain exterior and a magnificent interior.

Thomas Jefferson's **State Capitol**, Richmond, Virginia (1788–89) was very like the Maison Carrée in Nîmes in style, though it was much bigger. Jefferson had visited the Maison Carrée (and seen Palladian and Ancient Greek-style buildings in Paris) when he was the US ambassador in France.

Ancient Rome inspired Classical Palladian architecture.

1761 James Paine begins Kedleston Hall, Derbyshire, an elegant Neo-Classical building influenced by Palladio and Rome.

1761 Ange-Jacques Gabriel designs Petit Trianon, a well-propotioned Neo-Classical building, for Madame Pompadour in Versailles.

1766 onward James Graig begins work on Neo-Classical squares, terraces and crescents for the New Town in Edinburgh.

1771–82 Thomas Jefferson, future US president, creates a colonial-style home in Virginia.

ROMANTIC & REVOLUTIONARY
1770s – 1840s

In the Age of Romanticism, artists became the new heroes, reliving an idealised and fantastical past – of the exotic Eastern and Gothic worlds. In fact the Romantics plundered Chinese, Hindu, Islamic and medieval styles for their ideas.

The late 18th century was a time of great idealism. The United States rebelled against British rule in 1776. The French killed their king in 1789. New monumental architecture of pure, simple shapes captured this revolutionary spirit.

A scientific revolution in Europe and the USA was led by people like England's Isaac Newton, and coincided with an interest in Rationality or Reason. The Enlightenment tried to explain the world with science. Frenchman Diderot's *Encyclopedie* (1751), described the most up-to-date scientific thought.

THE GOTHIC REVIVAL
Neo-Gothic was a Victorian version of medieval Gothic architecture. This new style spread around the world.

St Pancras Hotel, London
Sir George Gilbert Scott designed this hotel in 1865 in a Victorian Gothic style.

ECCENTRIC
Some architects escaped into strange historical fantasy worlds blending Roman, Greek, Chinese and Indian styles to create eccentric buildings.

Edouard Riedel's and Georg von Dollmann's **Neuschwanstein** (1869–81) was a fairytale mountainside castle designed for mad Ludwig the 2nd of Bavaria, who pretended to be Lohengrin, the Swan Prince in the Wagner opera.

PICTURESQUE
Some architects thought that buildings or landscapes should create strong emotional reactions, like terror or astonishment. Darkness and gloom were especially popular.

The Industrial Revolution in Britain, France and Germany resulted from new scientific and technological ideas. Newly prosperous rich industrialists – the *nouveau riche* – spent money on fine, lavish architecture, which suited their extravagant tastes.

GREEK REVIVAL
The perfect classical temples of ancient Athens were the models for Greek Revival architecture. Architects even turned Edinburgh, Scotland into the 'Athens of the North'. In places like Prussia and North Germany, Greek Revival showed off the State's power.

John Nash designed the strange, picturesque, Indian-style **Royal Pavilion** in Brighton (1815–21).

George Edmund Street's **Royal Courts of Justice**, London (1874–82) showed all sorts of European 14th century Gothic touches.

Karl Friedrich Schinkel's **Altes Museum**, (1823–30) and **Schauspielhaus** (1819–21), both in Berlin, were working versions of Ancient Greek buildings.

The late 18th Century saw old styles revived and revolutionary architecture.

1807–45 Alexandre-Pierre Vignon designs Paris's Church of the Madelin, to Napoleon Bonaparte's taste.

1817–26 Thomas Jefferson designs the university library at Charlottesville to look like Rome's ancient Pantheon temple.

1825–29 Thomas Hamilton builds Edinburgh's Royal High School on a hill, like the Akropolis in Athens.

1861 In Ottawa, Fuller and Stent build Canada's Neo-Gothic style Parliament buildings.

HOUSES OF PARLIAMENT
London, England, 1836–68

Sir Charles Barry
(1785 –1860)

Augustus Pugin (1812–52)

Born in London, Barry toured Europe and the Middle East as a young man, drawing and studying architecture. His most famous building was the the Houses of Parliament, which he redesigned after it was destroyed by fire in 1834. But the project proved difficult because it ran late, and was well over budget.

On Barry's tombstone are some of his favourite Westminster designs.

Pugin, a strict Catholic and an energetic man, was a theatre set designer at Covent Garden before he began an architectural career. He loved to put colourful, detailed medieval-style decoration in his Gothic churches. He died insane aged only 40.

After the old timber Parliament building burned down in 1834, Sir Charles Barry won the competition to design a new one. This Parliament building had to hold both the House of Commons and Lords Chambers, as well as committee rooms, libraries and offices. It was an immensely important job – a national monument for a Victorian England that was the most powerful country in the world at that time.

Barry asked the brilliant designer, Pugin, to give the building Gothic detailing to blend in with the nearby Westminster Abbey and Westminster Hall. But the two men did not see eye-to-eye. Barry designed such a symmetrical, almost Classical building that Pugin complained it was all 'Tudor details on a classic body'. In the end, Pugin's intricate Gothic details ensured the building's popularity with the English people.

London's Houses of Parliament presented a many-towered Gothic skyline across the River Thames.

1853 P.C. Albert begins the rebuilding of Balmoral, Queen Victoria's Scottish castle.

1856 In Vienna, Heinrich von Ferste begins his ornately designed Votivkirche.

1858 Barry designs the third version of London's Covent Garden Opera House.

PARIS OPÉRA HOUSE
Paris, France, 1862–75

Jean-Louis-Charles Garnier (1825–1889)

Garnier's design for Paris Opéra was spectacular – a Roman temple, a palace and a cathedral, all rolled into one. Paris was a successful city and its greatness needed an opera house to match its high status. In 1864, Napoleon the 3rd established the *Ecole des Beaux Arts*, a national institution to encourage good French design.

Garnier's greatest commission, to design the Paris Opéra, was the centrepiece of a newly reorganised Paris. In the days when architects could choose to build in almost any style, Garnier chose to design a huge, colourful, ornate theatre, with an interior full of chandeliers, plaster and gold leaf.

Garnier thought that a theatre was a enchanted place, where the wealthy could watch and enjoy a magical spectacle on the stage and in the foyer. So it was important to make the opera house very grand and beautiful. Garnier covered the opera house with sculptures of composers and the Greek Muses, which represented dance and poetry. Inside, he made a huge stage with a majestic auditorium, entrance hall and Grand Staircase for the audience to see and be seen. Everywhere there were golden statues, painted ceilings and sparkling chandeliers.

Garnier was proud of his modern building. Inside, it had a lift, a ventilation system, a smoking room, a library, a doctor's surgery, a flower shop and even an ice-cream parlour.

Garnier's complicated and lavish Paris Opéra provided a centrepiece for a new city plan.

1862 Gilbert Scott designs the Albert Memorial in London, in honour of the dead Prince Regent.

1873 Semper designs a theatre, the Burgtheater, in Vienna.

1877 In Amsterdam, Pierre Cuypers builds the Rijksmuseum.

CHANGING CITIES
1750–1850

Catherine the Great (1729–96)

Catherine the Great was Empress of Russia from 1762–96 after her husband, Peter the Third's abdication and murder.

Franz Josef (1830–1916)

Emperor Franz Josef became the absolute ruler of Austria in 1848 and was proclaimed King of Hungary in 1867.

In 17th-century Europe, architects wanted to improve the look and grandeur of their cities. Backed by strong rulers, they had the power to make real progress. In the following centuries, Peter the Great and Catherine the Great in Russia – and Baron Haussmann in Paris – had the political will and power to push through even greater schemes that radically changed cities or even created them from scratch.

In the USA, architects laid out the new capital, Washington, in the swamps of Virginia.

ST PETERSBURG, RUSSIA

Peter the Great (1682–1725) looked westward from his Baltic ports for progressive ideas in all things, including architecture. He built St Petersburg as an entirely new city on the River Neva, beginning with the Peter-and-Paul fortress. Catherine the Great (1729–96) became Empress in 1762. Using Russia's huge wealth, she began to commission buildings and collect art to turn Russia into a modern European country and St Petersburg into an even grander city. Catherine liked French culture best, but she also used Russian, French, Scottish and Italian architectural designs.

1. New Admiralty
2. Emperor Catherine's Winter Palace (1754, Rastrellis)
3. Winter Palace Square
4. The Ministry of War (1819)

River Neva

River Danube

Ringstrasse

VIENNA, AUSTRIA

Emperor Franz Josef of Austria understood that a new centre of Vienna would make it easier to control if the population rebelled. In 1858 he had Vienna's old walls demolished, and replaced with Ludwig Förster's Ringstrasse. The emperor's army could reach any part of the city from this broad, curved avenue.

Ambitious rulers created new or improved capital cities in Europe and in the USA.

Early 18th century French architect, Le Blond, begins the Palace of Peterhof, St Petersburg, using Peter the Great's sketches. This summer palace had a modest study amongst the state apartments.

1747 Bartolomeo Rastrelli extends the Palace of Peterhof for Catherine the Great. The new building work included blocks and wings to look like a miniature Versailles Palace.

Louis Napoleon was the nephew of Napoleon Bonaparte. He was elected president of the Republic (in France) in 1848 and was proclaimed Emperor in 1852.

Napoleon the 3rd (1808–73)

George Washington (1732–99)

Washington was President of the USA from 1789–97. During that time the city named after him was founded in 1791.

PARIS, FRANCE

At the end of the 1840s, Napoleon Bonaparte's nephew proclaimed himself Napoleon the 3rd, at the head of France's Second Empire. His clever leadership made France a rich industrial country, and encouraged the 'tidying-up' of the medieval centre of Paris, under Baron Haussmann. Haussmann swept away small 'messy' buildings that got in the way of palaces and barracks – so that Napoleon's soldiers could easily control the city. Between 1853 and 1869 he replaced them with a 'Baroque' street pattern of 'rond-ponts' and broad radiating avenues, lined with 4- and 5-storeyed expensive apartments. Paris's centre-piece was the grand Paris Opéra.

PARIS

1. Notre Dame
2. The Pantheon
3. Les Invalides
4. Arc de Triomphe
5. Place de la Concorde
6. Paris Opéra House
7. The Louvre
8. Porte St. Denis
9. Place de la Republique
10. Place de la Bastille

WASHINGTON, USA

American leaders wanted a grand new version of classical architecture for their new capital. They thought of themselves as modern Greeks and Romans – cultures they so admired in the past. So the Frenchman, Pierre Charles l'Enfant (1754–1825), designed Washington with a layout like Paris's Versailles, but with its government buildings standing like classical Greek temples and monuments along the grand streets.

1. The Executive Mansion or President's House (White House)
2. The Capitol

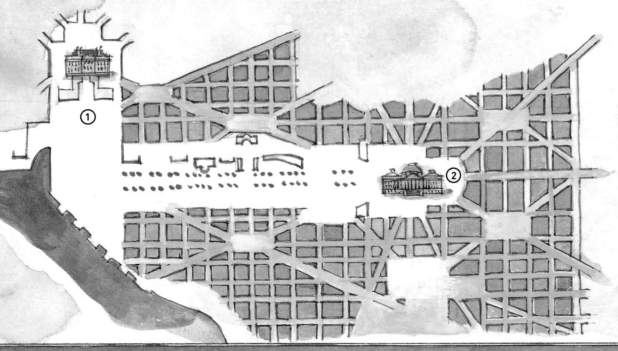

Only the most powerful rulers and states could achieve such sweeping changes.

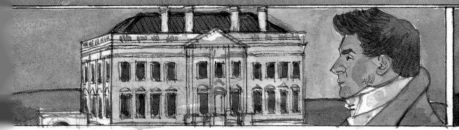

1792 James Hoban designs the first White House in Washington. The British burned it down in 1812.

1850s Georges Eugène Haussmann (1809–91) oversees the building of multi-storey apartments to line Paris's modernised wide, straight boulevards.

IRON AND THE INDUSTRIAL AGE
18th and 19th centuries

Before the 17th century, industry was based around farming. The Industrial Age was born when people learned how to smelt iron ore. Cities began to build factories that made iron machinery. Britain had good coal and iron reserves. Coal was used to power steam engines.

Steam power from coal could now be used by railways and ocean-going ships. Land and sea transport was much faster for people and cargo. The world's first mainline steam railway ran between Liverpool and Manchester in 1830.

The first iron bridge, Coalbrookdale, Shropshire
Before 1779, bridges were made of wood or stone. An iron bridge became possible when Abraham Darby the 3rd found a way to smelt iron ore using coke. His elegant bridge still spans the River Severn. More iron bridges were built to carry Britain's new roads.

Clifton Suspension Bridge, Bristol, 1829–63
Isambard Kingdom Brunel (1806–59) built this wrought iron suspension bridge over the steep Avon gorge. It had modern ironwork and Egyptian-style upright 'pylons' that were popular in the 19th century.

The Industrial Revolution began in England around 1780. It spread throughout Europe, reaching the south (Italy), east (Russia) and north (Sweden) as late as 1900. It began with the production of iron. Materials like iron and glass began to be mass produced and transported long distances. Engineers and architects saw the possibilities, and turned these modern materials into extraordinary and beautiful new structures.

Menai Strait Bridge, north-west Wales, 1819
For this bridge, Thomas Telford (1757–1834) used cast-iron, suspending the road-bed from metal chains. Only the towers used his customary masonry construction, here in an Egyptian style.

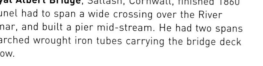

Royal Albert Bridge, Saltash, Cornwall, finished 1860
Brunel had to span a wide crossing over the River Tamar, and built a pier mid-stream. He had two spans of arched wrought iron tubes carrying the bridge deck below.

Britannia Railway Bridge, Menai Straits, 1850
Robert Stephenson (1803–59) built this bridge which spanned 300 metres (985 feet) over water. It had to be an inventive 'box girder' construction of wrought iron 'tubes' which carried the trains inside.

The Industrial Revolution ushered in new building methods still being exlored today.

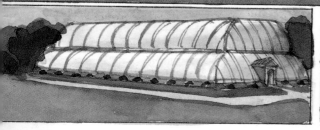

1836 Paxton designs a 90-metre-long (295 feet) conservatory at Chatsworth, Derbyshire.

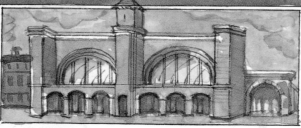

1850–52 Lewis Cubitt builds Kings Cross Station in yellow London brick, a beautiful and functional building with a double-span train shed behind.

1801 Thomas Telford designs an exciting bridge for London but it is never built.

Because the iron frame of the new industrial buildings carried the whole weight of the roof, the walls no longer had to be load-bearing. They could be delicate and thin. Architects also designed railway stations, some in classical styles with beautiful glass and iron train sheds.

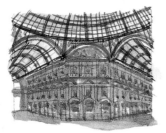

Galleria Vittorio Emanuele the 2nd
Milan, 1829/1865–67
Giuseppe Mengoni (1829–77)
This beautiful pedestrian street has iron and glass vaults and a dome over 19th century Milanese buildings.

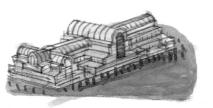

Crystal Palace, London Exhibition, 1851
Joseph Paxton (1801–65)
This massive glass and steel structure was 564 metres (1,850 feet) long, and used 300,000 plate glass sheets – none longer than 125 centimetres (49 inches). Yet it only took 2,000 men 3 months to build.

Gare de l'Est Paris, 1847–52
François-Alexandre Duquesney
Duquesney (1790–1849) built this Renaissance-style railway station. Its iron and glass shed had a span of over 30 metres (100 feet)!

Paddington Station London, 1852, I.K. Brunel (see page 42)
Railway stations were called the 'Cathedrals' of the Age. Brunel's shed had three wrought-iron framed spans, which were intersected by cross vaults.

Les Halles Centrales
Paris, begun 1853
Victor Baltard (1805–74)
This fruit and vegetable market had connected iron sheds roofed with glass and iron, and were spacious and light.

Oriel Chambers Liverpool, 1864
Peter Ellis (c. 1835–84)
This 5-storey office building had a cast-iron frame, but used it in a very ornate way.

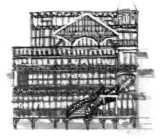

Magazins du Bon Marche
Paris, 1876, Gustave Eiffel (see page 45) & Louis-Charles Boileau (1812–96)
The huge space in this shopping arcade was lit naturally through a glass and iron roof. There were several shopping levels, cross-linked with bridges.

Galerie des Machines,
Paris Exhibition, 1889, Charles Dutert (1845–1906) with engineer Victor Contamin (1840–93)
This ambitious glass and steel exhibition space was huge – 430 by 120 metres (1,410 by 393 feet) and 45 metres (148 feet) high. It was the greatest span then built and looked like a huge bridge arch.

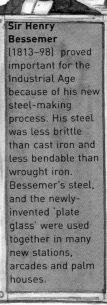

Victorian glass and steel structures paved the way for skyscraper buildings.

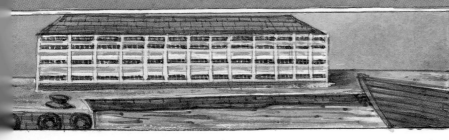

1858 G.T. Greene designs an architecturally advanced iron-framed boat store at the Sheerness navy dockyard.

1859–67 Like the earlier Bibliothèque St Genevieve (pictured), Labrouste's Bibliothèque Nationale has a beautiful, delicately-designed cast-iron frame.

John Roebling (1806-69)

BROOKLYN BRIDGE
New York, USA, 1867–83

Washington Roebling
(1837-1926)

John Roebling was born in Germany. He began the bridge in 1867 but in 1869 his foot was crushed between a ferry and the quay while overseeing the building work. John died three weeks later from tetanus. His son, Washington Roebling, took over from his father but was eventually taken from the site suffering from 'the bends', a terrible illness caused by nitrogen bubbles forming in the blood of divers. Many workers got this while labouring in caissons under the East River. This illness nearly killed him. Washington's wife, Emily, finally finished the bridge under his instructions.

Brooklyn Bridge spanned the East River, joining the cities of Manhattan and Brooklyn. Horse-drawn carriages used the two outer lanes. Cable cars travelled on the inside lanes, and pedestrians crossed on a central elevated walkway.

wire trusses

suspension cable

The spectacular Brooklyn Bridge, built over New York's East River, was a triumph of new engineering and new architecture. Its engineer, John Roebling, used super-modern steel suspension cables on his bridge – and he designed the masonry piers, sunk into the river-bed, in an imaginative mixture of ancient Egyptian, Roman and Gothic styles. Egypt symbolised strength, Rome represented civic greatness, and the Gothic reflected elegance. The bridge took 16 years to build because they had to build the piers below the river-bed. During constuction, over 20 workers lost their lives.

John Roebling hung his bridge's roadbed from the steel suspension cables, using thinner vertical wire. And, to make the bridge even stronger, he had diagonal wires stretched from the granite towers and along the roadway.

A double system of steel suspension cables held the enormous weight of Brooklyn Bridge's roadbed.

1846 Robert Stephenson's High Level railway bridge over the River Tyne, is one of the last cast-iron bridges.

1882–89 Sir Benjamin Baker builds the magnificent Forth Bridge in Scotland.

1884 Eiffel designs the 165-metre-long (541 feet) ironwork span for the Garabit Viaduct.

Alexandre Gustave Eiffel
(1832–1923)

EIFFEL TOWER

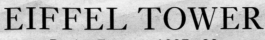

Paris, France, 1887–89

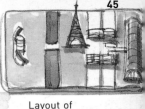

Layout of
the 1889 exhibition

Paris hosted its own Great Exposition in 1889, and the most eye-catching exhibit was the amazing, modern, 300-metre-high (984 feet) Eiffel Tower. The simple all-metal structure was the tallest in the world, and demonstrated how advanced French skills were in this kind of engineering. Eiffel's intention to impress the world succeeded.

By June 1887 the builders had finished preparing the tower's deep foundations. Then, using cranes and wooden scaffolding, they began construction on the tower's four legs, just as if they were bridge arches. Above the arches, the tower's tapering criss-cross metalwork design was there for strength and decoration. Each of the 12,000 iron pieces was prefabricated, then quickly and accurately riveted together on site. Everything was finished by April 1889, ready for the Exposition. The tower was strong and stable enough to withstand the very worst gales.

The Eiffel Tower still dominates Paris two centuries on – it is the city's most popular tourist destination. But it was not always so. In Eiffel's day most Parisians hated it, saying the tower ruined the city's skyline. And they said it was an insult to the cathedral and palaces that it dwarfed.

It took two and a half million rivets to hold the Eiffel Tower together. Because Parisians worried that the Tower might fall, extra ironwork was built in to convince them of its strength. This ironwork is only decoration – it isn't really needed.

Eiffel built the hidden steel skeleton or armature inside Bartholdi's Statue of Liberty sculpture. It gives New York's 91-metre-high (300 feet) landmark the strength to stand up.

At Paris' 1889 exposition, the Eiffel Tower and the Galerie des Machines were the greatest engineering exhibits.

1880 At long last, after 532 years, Cologne Cathedral is finished.

NEW YORK'S FIRST SKYSCRAPERS

Late 19th to early 20th centuries

Until Elisha Otis's Safety Elevator (1854) was invented, the highest building could only be 5 storeys high. This was because stone walls had to be thick to bear the whole weight of the building. When factories introduced production lines, it became cheaper to produce steel. Architects built strong, rigid steel frames high over deep foundations that could stand up by themselves. Because the frames were lightweight, the walls of these buildings could be thinner so the building could be higher.

Art Deco was a style of decoration in the 1920s and 30s that featured geometric shapes and bold colours. Examples can be found in many buildings of the time.

By the late 1800s, architects had devised a new way of building New York's big department stores, offices and factories. Recent inventions and factory mass-production had made exciting new skyscrapers possible, aided by a plentiful supply of money and solid ground. This vertical building style was perfect for a city like New York troubled by scarce and expensive land. The new multi-storey buildings had masonry walls hanging from rigid steel frames. As its buildings rose higher and higher, New York became a famous Skyscraper City.

① J.P. Gaynor's **Haughwout Store** (1856) was built in a 16th century Venetian style, but using prefabricated cast-iron sections bolted together – including its store front. In 1857, it had the first passenger lift in any town building.

② Richard M. Hunt's **Tribune Building** (1870s) was a very plain, undecorated building, 9 storeys and 80 metres (262 feet) high. It was one of the first true skyscrapers.

③ George B. Post's **Western Union Telegraph Building** (1873–75) is 10 storeys and 70 metres (230 feet) high.

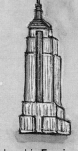

⑥ William Lamb's **Empire State Building** (1929–31) is a towering and elegant Art Deco skyscraper. During construction its steel frame was bolted and riveted together, then concrete was poured on to it. Next they fitted the windows and limestone cladding before laying the bricks. Finally the lifts were installed.

⑤ Cass Gilbert's **Woolworth Building** (1910–13) is 241 metre (791 feet) high. This popular skyscraper had terracotta cladding and Gothic decoratio over a steel frame. At 60 storeys it needed huge foundations at leas 17 metres (56 feet) deep

④ **The Park Row Building** (1899), with 36 storeys, was the world's highest building when it was constructed.

Early skyscrapers hid their steel frames under heavy, decorated masonry.

1871 A huge fire destroys thousands of timber-framed buildings in Chicago.

1873–86 The Great Western Railway Company builds a tunnel between England and Wales under England's River Severn estuary.

1879–84 Alexandre Gustave Eiffel builds the steel skeleton that holds up New York's Statue of Liberty.

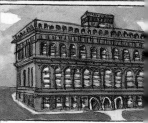

1881 George B. Post builds New York's Produce Exchange.

CHICAGO'S FIRST SKYSCRAPERS
Late 19th to early 20th centuries

Many of Chicago's buildings were timber-framed before the terrible fire of 1871, which wiped out much of the city. The awful destruction gave architects the chance to build a modern Chicago in steel. When the building boom made land expensive, they took advantage of new building materials, and up-to-the-minute inventions, to build upwards. Chicago became a skyscraper city, like New York.

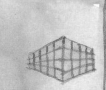

The work of the Chicago School of Architects (c.1850) looked to the future. There were three teams – Burnham and Root, Holabird and Roche and Adler and Sullivan. The older William Le Baron Jenney, and the imaginative Frank Lloyd Wright, were also very important Chicago architects.

The **Arts and Crafts** Movement reacted against buildings of the Machine Age. They believed that craftsmen should use local materials – definitely not metal frames – to create buildings untouched by modern industrial ways.

①
William Le Baron Jenney's **Home Insurance Building** (1884–85) had floors that were supported by the building's iron and steel frame. However, Jenney thought that the building's brick walls needed to support themselves – and so he built them thickly. Despite this, it was the first true skyscraper because of its strong, riveted, fire-proof steel frame.

②
William Holabird and Martin Roche's **Tacoma Building** (1887–89) had a steel frame that supported its floors and walls – another true skyscraper.

③
Dankmar Adler and Louis Sullivan's **Walker Warehouse** (1888–89) was a very modern-style building, though its masonry façade had a Classical look.

⑥
Burnham and Company's **Reliance Building** (1894–95) had 13 storeys, with very light curtain-wall cladding over its steel skeleton. The building's top 10 storeys were built in only 15 days!

⑤
Holabird and Roche's **Marquette Building** (1893–94) was a typical strong-looking Chicago building, built in a Classical style.

④
D.H. Burnham and J.W. Root's **Monadnock Building** (1891) was the last tall iron-framed building, at 7 storeys high, that had thick, load-bearing masonry walls.

The first true skyscrapers, in Chicago, hung their thin walls from rigid steel frames.

1893 In Illinois, Frank Lloyd Wright builds his new-style Winslow House.

1904 Holabird and Roche's West Jackson Boulevard Building rises in 20th-century Chicago.

1904-14 Eliel Saarinen designs and builds Helsinki's Central Railway Station using clear, simple shapes and lines.

Antoni Gaudì 1852–1926

The **Art Nouveau** style of decoration became popular at the end of the 19th century, especially for interiors, illustrations and jewellery.

In Paris, Hector Guimard (1867–1942) used the Art Nouveau style to design the curvy, plant-like cast-iron and wrought-iron entrances to the Métro.

SAGRADA FAMILIA
Barcelona, Spain, begun 1882

The Catalan architect, Antoni Gaudì, spent most of his later career working on just one project – the Sagrada Familia in Barcelona, Spain. Gaudì was very religious, and, inspired by God and Nature, this cathedral-like temple was his most precious work.

But still, a hundred years after building began, it remains unfinished. The Sagrada Familia is an extraordinary building, looking more like a growing, living thing than a building. Gaudì chose to create it in the Art Nouveau style he had already used in buildings like the Casa Batllo (the strange and animal-like building known as the House of Bones). Art Nouveau was an especially popular style in Barcelona, his beloved home city.

Over the Sagrada Familia's 100-metre-long (328 feet) nave rises a group of towers – the largest representing Christ. The four towers over the temple's western façade represent the 12 apostles.

The building shows off its colour, curves and rounded, organic shapes. Gaudì even made the tall, thin columns supporting the vaults inside, lean inwards – which makes them look like a stone forest.

Art Nouveau architecture was rarer than its art. But Gaudì designed the curvaceous-style homes at Park Güell (1900–14), the Casa Mila (1905–10) and Casa Batllo (1905–7) buildings.

Barcelona Catalans like Gaudì loved Art Nouveau's   flowery, flowing style.

1892–93 Victor Horta's Hotel Tassel, Brussels, is decorated with swirling paintings and mosaic designs.

1898–99 Otto Wagner creates an Art Nouveau façade for his Majolica House in Vienna.

1909 C.R. Mackintosh, the Scottish architect and designer, completes his Glasgow School of Art.

1920–21 Erich Mendelsohn builds the Art Nouveau-style Einstein Tower near Potsdam, Germany.

THE BAUHAUS
Germany, 1919–33

Walter Gropius founded Germany's Bauhaus School in Weimar in 1919. The school wanted to encourage modern, excellent and functional industrial design.

Relocating to Dessau in 1925, the 3-block Bauhaus Building contained workshops, classrooms and a 5-storey tower of studios and dormitories. Plain glass walls in the Bauhaus's workshops, and solid walled classrooms demonstrated the school's functional design.

When Hitler and his Nazi Party came to power in Germany, they detested the politics of the Bauhaus's brilliant, free-thinking students and teachers. They closed the school in 1933, and many of these exceptional people emigrated to America and became important architects there.

In 1908, Peter Behrens (1868–1940) designed the Classical-looking **AEG Turbine Factory** in Berlin. Some of Behrens's design assistants such as Gropius, Le Corbusier, and Mies van der Rohe were to become famous architects themselves.

The Fagus Factory (1911–13) Walter Gropius and Adolf Meyer designed the Fagus Factory at Alfeld-an-der-Leine in Germany, and began a fashionable functional style for factories all around the world.

Italian Futurists In 1914, two young architects, Antonio Sant'Elia and Mario Chiattone, made amazing futurist designs of a new city, **Citta Nuova**. Inspired by science and technology, the futurists wanted buildings to be light and practical. Nothing was built, but the two men's drawings and designs remain.

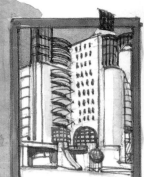

Dutch De Stijl artists (from 1917) wanted art and architecture to be central to people's lives. Aiming to design good Modern post-war housing – just as the Bauhaus did in Germany – they built several mass-housing schemes in Holland.

The Bauhaus designed modern functional buildings made of glass and steel.

1924 Gerrit Thomas Rietveld's famous Schroeder House is built in Utrecht, Holland.

1926–30 Karl Ehn's 'wall' of houses – the Karl-Marx-Hof in Vienna – contains flats, offices and many local services.

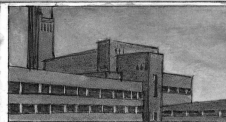

1926 Willem Marinus Dudok builds a modern town hall in Hilversum, Holland.

1930 J.F. Staal's multi-storey block of housing, the De Wlkenkrabbe is completed in Amsterdam, Holland.

William van Alen (1883–1954)

THE CHRYSLER BUILDING

New York, USA, 1928–30

The complete view of the Chrysler Building

Land prices continued to rise in 1920s New York. So did its skyscrapers – especially in the financial area around Wall Street.

The Chrysler Building was in East 42nd Street and for just one year, the 319-metre-high (1,047 feet), 77-storey grey and white brick skyscraper was the highest in the world. Cleverly, the architect William van Alen hid the skyscraper's 56 metre (184 feet) spire in its unfinished elevator shaft until the very last moment. Once in place, the Chrysler Building became 37 metres (121 feet) higher than New York's Bank of Manhattan!

Like many rival New York architects, van Alen had wanted to make his skyscraper a towering, modern and exciting building – just the right sort of headquarters for an ambitious car magnate like Walter Chrysler. Van Alen had chosen to decorate the building, inside and out, in the popular Art Deco style. In fact, the Chrysler Building became instantly famous for the triangular silver sunburst design on the stainless steel curves of its spire, and the metal eagles watching high over the New York streets.

Russian skyscrapers
In 1933, Boris Iofan, won the competition for Moscow's new 'Palace of the Soviets', designed as a 415 metre (1,365 feet) high building for government, educational and leisure use, topped with a 100-metre (325 feet) high statue of Lenin! But World War II arrived, so it was never built.

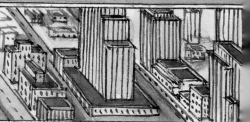

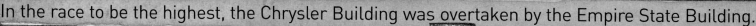

In the race to be the highest, the Chrysler Building was overtaken by the Empire State Building.

1903–13 New York's magnificent French-style Grand Central Station is designed.

1927–29 Konstantin Melnikov builds Rusakov Worker's Club in Moscow in the constructivist style.

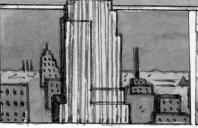

1930 Raymond M. Hood's futurist-looking Daily News Building in New York is totally unornamented.

1931–39 The Rockefeller Centre in New York groups city buildings and facilities around open spaces instead of using a single skyscraper.

Le Corbusier (1887–1965)

UNITÉ D'HABITATION
Marseille, France, 1946–52

1914 Domino House flexible construction

Machines for Living In
Le Corbusier wanted houses to work well – to be functional – and beautiful. He didn't intend that homes should actually be impersonal machines.

Le Corbusier, a Swiss whose real name was Charles-Eduoard Jeanneret, was a modern Renaissance Man and one of the most important architects of the 20th century. He was an artist, thinker and craftsman, as well as an architect of the Machine Age. Searching for ideas Le Corbusier toured Europe before settling in France and, in 1923, writing *Vers une Architecture* – a book outlining his views. He believed that modern architects should welcome a new industrial spirit. Buildings, he said, should be 'machines for living in'. This idea influenced architects all over the world. Le Corbusier's own Unité d'Habitation in Marseilles – a neighbourhood-in-a-block – was intended to live up to his beliefs.

It was a bold rectangular shape – a huge, modern, concrete, glass and steel housing-block lifted up on stilts called piloti. L'Unité held more than 300 apartments of varying sizes, and its 1,600 residents had all the facilities of a small town on their doorstep and rooftop.

With attention to detail, Corbusier created a shopping street within the building, sports facilities, and double-height living rooms – all intended to make the residents' lives as easy as possible.

side view of the Unité d'Habitation

Villa Savoye
Corbusier invented a system of proportions, just as architects in Classical Greece and Renaissance Italy had done. He wanted a home's proportions to be comfortable to live in, and look beautiful – like his white Villa Savoye, Poissy (1929–30)

In his Unité D'Habitation, Corbusier worked out how to house an entire community.

1946 Buckminster-Fuller designs the 'Wichita House' using aircraft assembly-line building techniques – an idea leading to his later Geodesic Domes.

1950–54 Le Corbusier designs a beautiful pilgrimage church, Notre-Dame-du-Haut, at Ronchamp, France.

1965 onwards Walter Segal perfects his ideas on cheap, easily constructed Self-Build homes.

Frank Lloyd Wright
1867-1959

GUGGENHEIM MUSEUM
New York, USA, designed 1943, built 1956–9

Falling Water (1936–39) Wright's most famous house, built in concrete, was designed to blend in with nature. It had strong horizontal 'cantilevered' balconies that stretched out over the water, and when Wright designed it for millionaire Edgar J. Kaufmann, he told him not to simply look at the waterfalls, but to live with them.

The famous American architect Frank Lloyd Wright began his career in Chicago in the 1890s, building beautiful, spacious homes for the rich. In his long life (he lived to be over 90) he designed many famous and original buildings. Perhaps the most eccentric was one of his last works, New York's Solomon R. Guggenheim Museum. It stands opposite New York's Central Park, like a futuristic spaceship tucked between Fifth Avenue apartment blocks. Wright's idea was to create a simple but unusual shape – a reinforced concrete shell, tapering downwards. Clinging to the shell's inside wall is a spiral walkway that grows wider as it climbs. This is where the museum hangs its paintings. On top of the whole curious structure, Wright put in a glass roof to let plenty of natural light in. Visitors take a lift to the top of the building, then walk slowly down the ramp, admiring the art. There are no pillars, columns or small gallery rooms to spoil their view. There aren't even windows looking out on to the New York streets!

The Guggenheim could never have been built without using structural, curved slabs of concrete. Concrete gave architects the freedom to design flowing, curved shapes. They first realised its possibilities in 1905, when Robert Maillart designed a reinforced concrete bridge in Felsegg, Switzerland.

Frank Lloyd Wright used concrete – a strong material capable of taking on interesting shapes.

1909–10 Wright's Robie House in Chicago opens up a new and original house style.

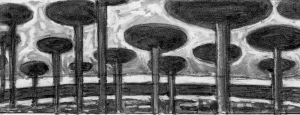

1936–39 Wright builds his Johnson Wax Building, Racine, with a glass roof.

1927 Richard Buckminster-Fuller perfects the prototype for Dymaxion House, an assembled machine for living in.

THE SYDNEY OPERA HOUSE
Sydney, Australia, 1957–73

Jorn Utzon (b. 1918)

So that all of the roof curves looked right together, Utzon made them up as pieces – or segments – of a single sphere.

It is really important that opera houses, concert halls and theatres are built so that the sound travels well inside. At first, Sydney Opera House's shell-shaped roof was very bad acoustically. To help, builders put in plywood and plexiglas surfaces inside the roof.

The Sydney Opera House design competition was won by the Danish architect Jorn Utzon, and looks as dramatic outside as its operas are inside. His design was selected in 1957 but the roof construction was beyond the capabilities of the engineers of that time. It was not until 1961 that the problem with the complex structure was solved. By 1966 there were many cost problems and the government almost stopped construction and Utzon angrily left the project.

Right on Sydney Harbour's waterfront, the building's roof is shaped like sails, or upturned boats, silhouetted against the sky. The engineers made the roof from pre-fabricated concrete ribs, strengthened with steel cables. Then they covered the whole roof with over a million brilliant ceramic tiles – and underneath, for light, put in huge amber-coloured glass windows. A concert hall and the opera theatre itself live in the two largest curving roof shells. The bottom of the building, a huge contrast to the soaring roof, is made of heavy-looking concrete and granite. Utzon built the base on to Sydney's sandstone bedrock at Bennelong Point, where it lies almost surrounded by water.

E qual via scegliete?

Individual architects' designs use new techniques and materials with great imagination.

1967 Richard Buckminster-Fuller's U.S. Pavilion at Expo '67 in Montreal develops his experimental, pre-fabricated dome structure, made of metal or plastic.

1969 Rogers and Piano design the Pompidou Centre, Paris, and bolt the services, such as the escalators, to the outside of the building.

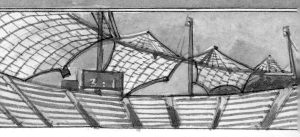

1972 Frei Otto's Olympic Games Tent, Munich, has huge spans and an umbrella roof made of a PVC-coated polyester fabric. It is held up by masts and cables.

WORLD HIGH RISES
1950s onwards

When Mies van der Rohe's Seagram Building was built in New York in 1954, another race began – to build the world's highest skyscraper. This time there was truly world-wide competition – not just American. But why did they build so high? In some cities, like New York, Tokyo and Hong Kong, land is scarce and expensive, and high buildings make sense. Some companies also want prestigious skyscrapers on their own, small, historic sites. But very often, such buildings are the proud boast of architects, clients, cities and even nations, showing off their engineering technology and wealth.

Engineers have had to learn even more sophisticated ways to make the world's vertical cities. Sometimes they design strengthened frames and skins of steel, or they hang the skyscraper's many storeys from a strong central core.

Seagram Building
(New York, 1954, Mies van der Rohe) Mies was a practical and ambitious architect who left Nazi Germany in the 1930s, and made his name in America. The Seagram Building was his best known skyscraper. It was a practical, functional and beautiful building, making use of the finest brass, marble, bronze, steel and glass.

John Hancock Center, (Chicago, 1965–70, Skidmore, Owings, Merrill and Khan) This tapered, 95-storey, 344 metre (1,129 feet) building overtook the Empire State Building as the world's highest. It was not just for corporate offices, people also lived, shopped and stayed there. Khan designed the centre with diagonal outside bracing, for strength against wind and earthquakes.

World Trade Center, (New York, 1966–73, Minoru Yamasaki) When these towers were added to the famous New York skyline, they were the world's highest, at 417 metres (1,368 feet). Their strength lay in their clever stressed skin made of steel mesh, unfortunately not strong enough to withstand the terrorist attacks of September 11th 2001.

Sears Tower, (Chicago, 1974, Fazlur Khan and Bruce Graham) The 442-metre-high (1,450 feet) Sears Tower was constructed using bundles of 'tubes'. Though not a beautiful building, it was still the world's highest for 20 years!

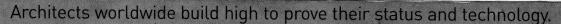

Architects worldwide build high to prove their status and technology.

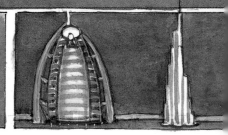

1933 Frank Lloyd Wright plans a 'half-mile-high' building to hold all Chicago's World Fair.

1947 The 39-storey U.N. Secretariat Building is built in New York on a site donated by J.D. Rockefeller Jr.

1966 Oscar Niemeyer's National Congress Building in Brasilia is one of his many designs in Brazil's modern capital.

1970s Architects build Islamic-style skyscrapers in the Middle East.

Earthquakes and typhoons
Places like Japan and Taiwan have to deal with even more dangers when they build skyscrapers. The countries lie in typhoon and earthquake belts, and their modern buildings are specially strengthened to withstand the forces of nature.

Skyscraper Safety
After the terrible attacks on New York's World Trade Center's twin towers, architects and engineers have reassessed the safety of skyscrapers. The towers were built to be tin tubes with open floors. Experts believe the floor supports burnt due to the fire, causing each floor to collapse on to the one below. Engineers designing skyscrapers now include better fire proofing, a concrete core, and a plan to evacuate people very quickly.

Burj Dubai
(Dubai, Skidmore, Owings and Merrill)
Designed by New York architects, if it is built, this 800-metre-high (2,625 feet) skyscraper will streak ahead of the race, and become the world's highest skyscraper!

Freedom Tower
(a design to replace the World Trade Center, New York – Daniel Liebeskind) Liebeskind won a bitterly-fought competition to fill the site of the World Trade Center. His tower will soar above a group of lower buildings, and it will be a significant 1,776 feet (541 metres) high, representing the year America declared its independence.

Taipei 101
(Taiwan, 2004, C.Y. Lee and C.P. Wang)
The finished 508 metre (1,667 feet), 101-storey building was planned to be the world's tallest and strongest skyscraper. Engineers say it can withstand the impact of a jumbo jet. Because of its height, the tower has very fast lifts, taking passengers to the top floor in just 39 seconds! C.Y. Lee designed it in Asian style, bamboo-like, dividing it into 8 sections. Eight is a Chinese lucky number and bamboo symbolises Taiwan's strong, fast-growing economy.

Shanghai World Financial Centre
(Shanghai, 1997–2001, Kohn Pederson Fox)
This 492-metre-high (1,614 feet) tower, designed in 1997, is still one of the highest buildings in the world. The huge hole at its top is both beautiful and practical as it reduces wind resistance.

Petronas Tower,
(Kuala Lumpur, 1992–7, Cezar Pelli)
Malaysia's 452-metre-high (1,483 feet) twin pagoda towers were the world's highest building at the time, and were deliberately Asian in appearance.

Terrorist attacks and natural disasters are risks for modern skyscrapers.

1979–86 Norman Foster's Hong Kong and Shanghai Bank is a tower on Hong Kong's skyline.

1985–90 I.M. Pei, Cobb, Freed and Partners build a towering skyscraper in Hong Kong, for the Bank of China.

1989–93 Jean Nouvel designs a cylindrical 'Tour Sans Fins' – a never-ending tower – for Paris.

1993–98 The 88-storey Jin Mao Tower in Shanghai is built according to Chinese feng shui ideas.

Robert Venturi (b. 1925)

POSTMODERN BUILDINGS
mid-1960s to today

Venturi's first book, *Complexity & Contradiction in Architecture*, became popular because many people wanted the end of awful skyscrapers. In a second book, *Learning from Las Vegas*, Venturi and his wife Denise Scott Brown attacked the ideas of Modernist architecture. They said that the many symbols seen in Las Vegas's messy streets – its signs, billboards, neon pictures, fake Classical statues, and so on – were what made it a lively place to be. They believed that new architecture should not forget this liveliness.

A number of architects working in the mid-1960s grew tired of identical international city-centres – full of dull, slab-like, modern skyscrapers. They could see that interesting old communities were being torn down, only to be replaced with boring shopping malls and office blocks. One architect, Robert Venturi, decided to take action. He demanded complicated, messier, livelier and more enjoyable city architecture. This was part of a movement called Postmodernism. Postmodern skyscrapers were designed with a bottom, middle and a top, like Johnson's AT&T Building (1978–83), nicknamed 'the Chippendale Skyscraper' because the top looked like a piece of the famous furniture!

Teatro del Mondo
Aldo Rossi (1931–97)
(Venice, Italy, 1979)
Rossi began a fight-back against Italy's post-World War II political and architectural chaos. He did it by stressing extreme order, not with the messiness favoured by his fellow architects. The Teatro del Mondo, a temporary, colourful wooden theatre for the 1980 Venice Bienniale – afloat on a barge – was an example of this orderliness.

Public Services Building
Michael Graves (b. 1934)
(Portland, USA, 1980–2)
Resembling a stage design with its imaginative mixture of colours and materials, this cube-shaped building used ideas from the revolutionary 18th century French architect, Ledoux.

Vanna Venturi House
Robert Venturi, (b.1925)
(Philadelphia, USA, 1962)
Built for his mother, this house seemed like a typical American home with a porch – but it also re-worked ideas about proportion and architecture put forward by the 16th century architect Palladio, and Le Corbusier in the 20th century.

Piazza d'Italia
Charles Moore (1925–93)
(New Orleans, USA, 1975–80)
Moore was interested in architectural history and in creating a 'sense of place'. This piazza – or square – had an Italian-American sense of place in its eccentric use of colour, Classical Roman ideas, water, statues – and even a 3D map of Italy!

Neue Staatsgalerie & new chamber theatre
James Stirling (1926–92) & Michael Wilford (b. 1938)
(Stuttgart, Germany, 1977–84)
This German gallery was a clever mix of Classical ideas and colourful Postmodern design. In a difficult city site next to an older gallery, Stirling combined the old and the new in a fresh and interesting way, using historical details and modern technology.

Postmodern architects wanted to make cities interesting places to live.

1965–74 Charles Moore builds a bright and lively dormitory complex for Kresge College in Santa Cruz, California.

1970s Robert Stern works on a storefront for Best Products Inc. in Maryland, USA, using ancient Classical orders.

1976–78 SITE (Sculpture in the Environment) design an amusing building – the Tilt Showroom of Best Products Inc.

1983–89 Pei, Cobb, Freed and Partners use a glass pyramid design for the entrance to the Louvre Museum in Paris

CONTEMPORARY AND BEYOND

Frank Gehry (b. 1929)

Renzo Piano (b. 1937)

Today half the world's population live in cities. In future, architects will have to use their skills to build smart, efficiently engineered buildings. At the same time, most architects will want to make their buildings eco-friendly, connecting them to the natural world. Some architects might recycle old buildings, giving them a new life instead of demolishing them.

Most cities grow in an unplanned way – invaded both by cars and international-style buildings like skyscrapers and stadiums. If wealthy people move to the suburbs, city centres can become derelict and unpleasant. But with careful planning, modern cities, like Barcelona, can be really enjoyable places to live. Future cities must follow their example.

Bankside Power Station, London (c. 2000)
Originally by Giles Gilbert Scott, reworked by Swiss architects Herzog (b. 1950) and De Meuron (b. 1950) into today's **Tate Modern** gallery.

From the 1960s to the present day, industrial development has destroyed many fine old buildings, only to replace them with much poorer ones. A few architects have fought against this waste, reusing the best old buildings and combining old and new in one space.

Ecological Building (2004), Emilio Ambasz. Ecological Architecture is a way of creating sustainable communities that work in harmony with the Earth's biosphere, not against it. So, an eco-tower or pyramid must be heated by the sun, cooled by evaporation and use power and water extremely efficiently. In such a 'living' building, waste must be recycled, and rain must be collected for plants and also recycled for drinking. Buildings now on the drawing board intend to make the natural and built environment blend together to leave little impact on local ecology.

Co-Existence Research Project, New York and London (1985)
This optimistic Future Systems project was very influential in its day. It demonstrated a new way of creating a tower for mixed uses (eg offices, residential and leisure) – a Mother Structure of self-contained communities in the sky. Space Age research has brought about modular structures. They are repeatable and very adaptable – perfect for self-contained communities like space stations, moon bases, giant orbiting 'mother-structures' – or towers here on Earth.

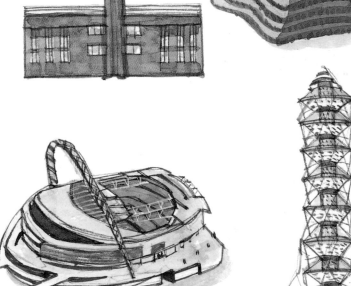

Wembley Stadium (2007)
Begun in 2002 by the World Stadium team of architects, the finished National Stadium will hold over 90,000 spectators comfortably in steep tiers of seats, all with unobstructed views. The landmark Wembley arch, 133 metres high (436 feet), will support Wembley's sliding roof.

Future architects must make cities good places to live in.

1991–97 Frank O'Gehry's unusual Guggenheim museum in Bilbao, Spain, looks like a sculpture.

1998 Renzo Piano finishes his Jean-Marie Tjibaou Cultural Centre using natural curved structures made of steel, glass and timber.

1998 Nicholas Grimshaw designs giant linked bio-dome greenhouses in Cornwall's quarries, to house diverse plants in the 'Eden Project'.

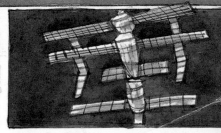

1998 onwards Work continues on the International Space Station, as it orbits 131 kilometres (210 miles) above the Earth.

Glossary

Abdication   when a monarch gives up his or her throne.

Akropolis   a high fortified part of an ancient Greek city such as Athens. It is also sometimes spelled Acropolis.

Ambulatory   an aisle for walking along, usually in a church or monastery.

Amphitheatre   usually an unroofed circular building or stadium, for contests and spectacles, where tiers of seats surround a central space called an arena.

Anatomy   the study or science of the inside structure of a plant or animal.

Aqueduct   a man-made channel, usually on a bridge, for carrying water across a valley.

Arcade   a series of arches held up on piers (large, square vertical supports) or columns.

Architect   a designer of buildings who prepares plans and supervises construction.

Art Deco   a decorative, geometrical style, fashionable in the 1920s and 30s, which relied on fine workmanship and materials. The style was used in architecture, furniture and jewellery design.

Art Nouveau   an artistic and architectural style at the turn of the late 19th and early 20th centuries, characterised by the flowing, organic lines of stylised plants and animals.

Asia Minor   a peninsular in the westernmost part of Asia, taking in most of Turkey, and bounded by the Black, Aegean and Mediterranean seas.

Auditorium   the part of a theatre where the audience sits.

Balustrade   a railing supported by 'balusters' - ornamental short pillars.

Basilica   originally a large rectangular public building in ancient Rome, with a central nave and side aisle. It is also a long Christian church with a similar form.

Bio-Dome   a modern, man-made dome structure, most often built to hold diverse communities of plants.

Biosphere   the parts of the Earth's crust and atmosphere where living organisms live.

Boulevard   a broad tree-lined street or road.

Box Girder   a type of bridge construction that uses a hollow girder and has a square cross-section.

Britannia   a helmeted woman, holding a shield and trident, who from Roman times became the personification of Britain.

Buttress   a structure that gives support to the outside of a building. A flying buttress is a supporting arch through two floors connected to the upper part of the building or roof.

Byzantine   the area that was the eastern part of the Roman Empire, after it was divided in AD 395. Its capital became Byzantium, now Istanbul.

Cantilever   a long bracket or beam fixed at one end (like on a vertical pier on a bridge), which projects from a structure.

Classical   usually relating to the art, literature, culture, or architecture of Ancient Greece or Rome.

Coke   what is left of coal after the gasses have been removed. It is used in blast furnaces to produce molten iron.

Colonnades   a row of columns, often supporting a roof in Classical architecture.

Commission   a group of people entrusted to perform certain tasks or duties.

Cupola   a rounded dome.

Eco-Friendly   not harmful to the natural environment.

Façade   the main outside face of a building, usually at the front.

Follies   costly ornamental buildings that have no practical use.

Fresco   a watercolour painting made on a wall or ceiling while the plaster is still wet.

Frieze   a horizontal band, often decorated with sculpture or painting, and found in Classical architecture.

Functional   in architecture, buildings designed to be practical rather than decorative or attractive.

Geodesic Dome   a dome made from short struts, and constructed in a semi-circle shape.

Geometry   a branch of mathematics that deals with points, lines, surfaces and solids, and how they relate to one another.

Gothic   a style of architecture popular in Europe from the 12th century and characterised by pointed windows, rose windows, rib-vaulting and flying buttresses.

Greek Muses   in Greek mythology, the nine goddesses, daughters of Zeus, who inspired the arts and sciences.

Guild   a group of people who associate to help each other, or share a common goal, often medieval craftsmen.

Ice Age   a geological period when glacial ice spread over large areas of the Northern Hemisphere, beginning c. 2 million years ago and ending c. 12,000 years ago.

Imperial   magnificent and majestic, having the characteristics of an emperor or an empire.

Industrial Revolution   (c. 1750-1850) the change from an agricultural to an industrial economy. Britain pioneered this in the mid-18th century, with new inventions in steam power leading to textile factories, steam railways and rapidly increasing wealth from manufacturing.

Labyrinth   a network of passages, like a maze. It was originally where the mythical half-man, half-bull Minotaur lived in ancient Crete.

Lintel   the horizontal supporting piece (usually stone or wood) across the top of a door or window, or other vertical structure.

Load-Bearing   a structure such as a wall which carries the weight of the building so is vital to the building's safety and stability.

Machicolations   a defensive construction projecting out from the top of a medieval building or tower. Hot liquids and missiles can be hurled from openings in the floor.

Mason   a builder who works with stone.

Mass-Production   the making of a standard item in very large quantities using a mechanised factory process.

Mastaba   a simple bench-like ancient Egyptian tomb, with a flat roof and sloping sides, and a passageway leading to an underground tomb.

Medieval   the Middle Ages of Europe, between ancient and modern times, approximately between the 5th and 15th centuries.

Mesoamerica   the thin strip of land and countries between the large South and North American continents. It is also called Central America.

Minaret   a thin turret or tower at a mosque, from which men called muezzin call people to prayer at certain hours of the day.

Modernism   the modern fashion in art and architecture, which began in the 20th century.

Mosaic   small coloured pieces of glass or stone, arranged to make a picture or pattern.

Nave   the long central space of a church, from the main western entrance to the area where the 'transept' arms cross it at right angles.

Obelisk   a tapering, four-sided stone pillar or monument.

Organic   in art and architecture, forms and styles derived from plant and animal shapes.

Pagan   someone not belonging to one of the main world religions.

Pagoda   a Hindu or Buddhist temple, often a many-tiered tower, often found in India, China and Japan.

Palm Houses   large greenhouses built in the 19th century from iron and glass, to house palm plants and trees.

Pavilion   a decorative building, often in a garden, or a building used for entertainments.

Pedestrian   related to walking, a place where only walkers, not motorists, are allowed.

Pediment   a triangular front of a Classical-style building, above the portico (entrance porch) of columns.

Perspective   a system of drawing, invented in early 15th century Italy, where real or imaginary lines give the illusion of distance and 3-dimensional depth on a 2-dimensional surface.

Pier   a large vertical support, usually rectangular in its cross-section, used in bridge construction.

Plinth   in architecture, the square slab under a column, or the base which supports a statue.

Postmodernism   a late 20th-century name for designs which rejected Modernism's pure forms and techniques. Postmodern architects used a mixture of past styles, and also used ornament, colour and sculpture - sometimes humorously.

Prefabricate   to make sections (eg of a building) at one location, before assembling them at the finished site.

Prototype   an original thing which is the model from which copies or improvements are made.

Reformation   the religious movement of the 16th century which broke away from the Catholic Church and led to the establishment of the Protestant Church.

Renaissance   a renewed interest in art, architecture, literature and Thought which happened in Europe in the 14th to 16th centuries, using Classical Greek and Roman ideas.

Rib-vaulting   a curved stone or timber structure which supports a roof. Fan-vaulting is a variation of rib-vaulting.

Rivet   one of a series of nails or bolts that hold metal plates together.

Romanesque   a European style of architecture from the 11th and 12th centuries characterised by heavy walls and arches, and a basilica shape.

Sanctuary Roof   the roof of the sanctuary and the holiest place in a temple.

Sarcophagus   a stone coffin.

Sculpture   the art of making 3-dimensional forms by carving, chiselling or casting stone, clay or wood.

Serf   a labourer not allowed to leave the land on which he works.

Settlement   the colonisation of an area, or the actual place that people have settled.

Shrine   a place, such as a chapel or altar, which is sacred.

Slave   someone who is the legal property of another person.

Smelting   the extraction of metal from rock or ore by melting it at high temperatures.

Stone Age   a prehistoric period when weapons and tools were made from stone.

Storey   all the rooms in a building that are on one floor. There may be several storeys to the building.

Sumerian   someone living in Sumer, an ancient civilisation and a district of Babylon, in Mesopotamia.

Surveyor   a person who views a building's condition and measures land.

Suspension Cable   thick wires hanging from tall pier structures on a bridge, which support the suspended roadway.

Symmetry   a structure that, even after being divided, has parts of equal shape and size. A symmetrical structure usually appears to be very well balanced.

Tetanus   a potentially fatal bacterial disease that makes muscles rigid and likely to suffer spasms. It is sometimes called 'lockjaw'.

Tomb   a large underground vault or space where the dead are buried.

Transept   the arms of a cross-shaped church, built at right angles to the long nave.

Urban Revolution   an historical time beginning thousands of years ago when people began to leave farming for the city to specialise in other skills. They built towns and created more complex class and social systems.

Vault   an underground chamber, or a continuous arch or series of arches, built in brick or stone.

Ventilation   the free circulation of fresh air into and out of a room.

Vista   a long, narrow view, sometimes between rows of trees or buildings.

Whitewash   a mixture of ground chalk and quicklime, which is used to whiten walls and ceilings.

Ziggurat   a rectangular, stepped tower topped with a temple, usually found in Mesopotamia.

Index

Abbey Church at Cluny, The 18
Abbey Church at Ottobeuren 31
Abbey of St Denis, The 19
Adler, Dankmar 47
AEG Turbine Factory 49
Akropolis, The 13, 37
Albert Memorial, The 39
Albert, P.C. 38
Alberti, Leon Battista 22, 23
Alen, William van 50
Alhambra, The 21
Altes Museum 37
Ambasz, Emilio 57
Amiens Cathedral 20
Ananda Temple at Pagan, The 17
Angkor Wat 17
AT&T Building 56

Baker, Benjamin 44
Baldacchino 31
Balmoral 38
Baltard, Victor 43
Bank of China Tower 55
Bank of Manhattan 50
Bankside Power Station 57
Banqueting Hall at Whitehall 27
Baptistry at Piza 18
Barelli, Agostino 33
Barma 26
Barry, Charles 38
Bauhaus Building 49
Behrens, Peter 49
Bell Tower of Ivan the Terrible, The 26
Bernini, Gian Lorenzo 24, 30, 31, 32, 34
Bessemer, Henry 43
Best Products Inc 56
Bibliothèque Nationale 43
Bibliothèque St Genevieve 43
Blond, Jean-Baptiste Alexandre le 40
Boffrand, Germain 31
Boileau, Louis-Charles 43
Borromini, Francesco 30
Bramante, Donato 22, 23, 24
Britannia Railway Bridge 42
Brooklyn Bridge 44
Brunel, Isambard Kingdom 42, 43
Brunelleschi, Filippo 22
Buckminster-Fuller, Richard 51, 52, 53
*Buddhist 'Temple Mountain'
  at Borobudur, The* 17
Buon, Bartolomeo 21
Buon, Giovanni 21
Burghley House 23
Burgtheater 39

Burj Dubai 55
Burlington, Lord 36
Burnham, Daniel 47

Cambio, Arnolfo di 21
Campen, Jacob van 33
Canterbury Cathedral 19
Carnac, The Standing Stones at 10
Casa Batllo 48
Casa Mila 48
Castle Howard 34
Cathedral of the Dormiton, The 23
Cecil, William 23
Central Railway Station, Helsinki 47
Chateau des Maisons 30
Chateau of Anet, The 26
Chatsworth, Conservatory at 42
Chiattone, Mario 49
Chichén Itzà 29
Chiswick House 36
Christ Church in Spitalfields 34
Chrysler Building, The 50
Church of the Madelin, The 37
Citta Nuova 49
Clifton Suspension Bridge 42
Cloth Hall, The 21
Co-Existence Research Project 57
Cobb, Henry N. 55, 56
Cologne Cathedral 45
Colosseum, The 14, 23
Contamin, Victor 43
Corbusier, Le 49, 51, 56
Cornaro Chapel 32, 35
Covent Garden Opera House 38
Crystal Palace 43
Cuypers, Pierre 39

Daily News Building 50
Darby, Abraham the 3rd 42
De Wlkenkrabbe 49
Doge's Palace, The 21, 25
Dollmann, Georg von 37
Dome of the Rock, The 16
Domino House 51
Dudok, Willem Marinus 49
Duomo, The 21, 22
Duquesney, François-Alexandre 43
Durham Cathedral 18
Dutert, Charles 43
Dymaxion House 52

Ecological Building 57
Eden Project, The 57
Ehn, Karl 49

Eiffel, Alexandre Gustave 43, 44, 45
Eiffel Tower, The 45
Einstein Tower 48
Ellis, Peter 43
Empire State Building, The 46, 50
Escorial Palace 25

Fagus Factory, The 49
Falling Water 52
Felsegg Bridge 52
Ferste, Heinrich von 38
Fiumi 31
Florence Cathedral (see *Duomo, The*)
Floris, Cornelius 25
Förster, Ludwig 40
Forth Bridge 44
Foster, Norman 55
Fox, Kohn Pederson 55
Freed, James Ingo 55, 56
Freedom Tower 55
Fuller, Thomas 37

Gabriel, Ange-Jacques 36
Galerie des Glaces 33
Galerie des Machines 43, 45
Galleria Vittorio Emanuele the 2nd 43
Garabit Viaduct 44
Gare de l'Est 43
Garnier, Jean-Louis-Charles 39
Gaudì, Antoni 48
Gaynor, J.P. 46
Geodesic Domes 51
Gesu Church, Il 22
Gilbert, Cass 46
Glasgow School of Art 48
Globe, The 27
Graham, Bruce 54
Graig, James 36
Grand Central Station 50
Graves, Michael 56
Great Mosque at Sammara, The 16
Great Mosque in Delhi, The 35
Great Mosque of Cordoba, The 16
Great Wall of China, The 13
Great Wall of Uruk, The 12
Greene, G.T. 43
Grimshaw, Nicholas 57
Gropius, Walter 49
Guarini, Guarino 30
Guggenheim Museum (Bilbao), The 57
Guggenheim Museum (New York), The 52
Guimard, Hector 48

Hadrian's Wall 10

Hagia Sophia — 15
Half-Mile-High Building — 54
Hall of a Hundred Columns, The — 11
Halles Centrales, Les — 43
Hamilton, Thomas — 37
Hampton Court Palace — 27
Hanging Gardens of Babylon, The — 11
Haughwout Store — 46
Haussmann, Georges Eugene — 40, 41
Hawksmoor, Nicolas — 34
Herrera, Juan de — 25
Herzog, Jacques — 57
High Level Railway Bridge — 44
Hoban, James — 41
Holarbird William — 47
Home Insurance Building — 47
Hong Kong and Shanghai Bank — 55
Hood, Raymond M. — 50
Horta, Victor — 48
Hotel de Soubise — 31
Hotel Tassel — 48
Houses of Parliament, The — 38
Hunt, Richard M. — 46

Iktinos — 13
Imhotep — 12
International Space Station, The — 57
Iofan, Boris — 50
Iron Bridge at Coalbrookdale, The — 42
Ishtar Gate — 13

Jean-Marie Tjibaou Cultural Centre — 57
Jeanneret, Charles-Eduoard (see Corbusier, Le)
Jefferson, Thomas — 36, 37
Jenney, William Le Baron — 47
Jew's House, The — 20
Jin Mao Tower — 55
John Hancock Center — 54
Johnson Wax Building — 52
Johnson, Philip — 56
Jones, Inigo — 27, 34

Ka'ba, The — 16
Kallikrates — 13
Karl-Marx-Hof — 49
Karlskirche — 31
Kedleston Hall — 36
Khan, Fazlur — 54
Kings Cross Station — 42
Knossos, The Palace at — 12
Kresge College — 56
Kubbet es-Sakhra (see *Dome of the Rock, The*)

L'Enfant, Charles — 41

L'Orme, Philibert de — 23, 26
Labrouste, Henri — 43
Lamb, William — 46
Leaning Tower of Piza, The — 18
Lee, C.Y. — 55
Lescot, Pierre — 25
Library of San Marco, The — 22, 23
Liebeskind, Daniel — 55
Lighthouse of Alexandria, The — 13
Little Moreton Hall — 27
Lombardo, Pietro — 23
Longhena, Baldassare — 30
Louvre Museum Glass Pyramid, The — 56
Louvre Palace — 25, 34
Luzarches, Robert de — 20

Mackintosh, C.R. — 48
Magazins du Bon Marche — 43
Maillart, Robert — 52
Maison Carree — 36
Majolica House — 48
Mansart, Francois — 30
Mansart, Jules Hardouin — 33, 34
Marquette Building — 47
Mathey, J.B. — 33
Mayan Temple of the Great Jaguar, The — 15
Melnikov, Konstantin — 50
Menai Strait Bridge — 42
Mendelsohn, Erich — 48
Mengoni, Giuseppe — 43
Merrill, John — 54, 55
Métro entrances (Paris), The — 48
Meuron, Pierre de — 57
Michaelangelo — 22, 24
Monadnock Building — 47
Moore, Charles — 56
Moro — 31

Nash, John — 37
National Congress Building — 54
Neue Staatsgalerie & New Chamber Theatre — 56
Neuschwanstein — 37
Niemeyer, Oscar — 54
Nonsuch Palace — 27
Notre Dame Cathedral — 20
Notre, Andre le — 33
Notre-Dame-du-Haut — 51
Nouvel, Jean — 55

O'Gehry, Frank — 57
Olympic Games Tent in Munich, The — 53
Orford Castle — 20
Oriel Chambers — 43
Otto, Frei — 53

Owings, Nathaniel — 54, 55

Paddington Station — 43
Paine, James — 36
Palace of Peterhof, The — 40
Palace of the Soviets, The — 50
Palace of Versailles, The — 31, 33, 34, 40
Palazzo Chiericati — 25
Palazzo Farnese — 23, 24
Palazzo Pubblico — 21
Palazzo Vecchio — 21
Palladio, Andrea — 23, 24, 25, 26, 34, 36, 56
Panthéon in Paris, The — 36
Pantheon Temple, The — 14, 37
Paris Opera House — 39
Park Guëll — 48
Park Row Building, The — 46
Parliament Buildings in Canada, The — 37
Parthenon, The — 13, 35
Paxton, Joseph — 42, 43
Pearl Mosque, The — 35
Pei, I.M. — 55, 56
Pelli, Cezar — 55
Perikles — 13
Persepolis — 11
Peruzzi, Baldassare — 23, 24
Petit Trianon — 36
Petronus Tower — 55
Piano, Renzo — 53, 57
Piazza d'Italia — 56
Piazza del Popolo — 32
Piazza Navona — 31
Piazza of St Peter (see *St Peter's Piazza*)
Pillar Temple, The — 11
Pisa Cathedral — 18
Pompidou Centre — 53
Pont du Gard — 14
Poppelmann, Matthaus Daniel — 31
Porta, Giacomo della — 22
Post, George B. — 46, 47
Postnik — 26
Potala Palace — 33
Poznan Town Hall — 23
Produce Exchange in New York — 46
Public Services Building — 56
Pugin, Augustus — 38
Pyramids at Giza, The — 11, 12

Quadro, Giovanni Battista — 23

Rainaldi, Carlo — 32
Raphael — 24
Rastrelli, Bartolomeo — 40
Red Fort — 35

Redentore, Il	22, 25	
Reliance Building	47	
Riedel, Edouard	37	
Rietveld, Gerrit Thomas	49	
Rijksmuseum	39	
Robie House	52	
Roche, Martin	47	
Rochester Castle	18	
Rockefeller Centre, The	50	
Roebling, Emily	44	
Roebling, John	44	
Roebling, Washington	44	
Rogers, Richard	53	
Rohe, Mies van der	49, 54	
Root, J.W.	47	
Rose Theatre, The	27	
Rossi, Aldo	56	
Royal Albert Bridge	42	
Royal Circus	36	
Royal Courts of Justice	37	
Royal Crescent	36	
Royal High School	37	
Royal Pavilion	37	
Rusakov Worker's Club	50	
Saarinen, Eliel	47	
Sacsahuaman	29	
Sagrada Familia	48	
Salisbury Cathedral	19	
San Carlo alle Quattro Fontaine	30	
San Giorgio Maggiore	25	
San Vitale Church	15	
Sangallo, Antonio da	23, 24	
Sansovino, Jacopo	23	
Sant'Andrea	22, 23	
Sant'Andrea al Quirinale Church	32	
Sant'Ella, Antonio	49	
Santa Maria dei Miracoli	22, 23, 32	
Santa Maria dei Monte Santo	32	
Santa Maria della Consolazione	23	
Santa Maria della Salute	30	
Santa Maria della Vittoria	32, 35	
Santa Maria Novella	22, 23	
Scala Regia	32	
Schauspielhaus	37	
Schinkel, Karl Friedrich	37	
Schroeder House	49	
Scott, George Gilbert	37, 39	
Scott, Giles Gilbert	57	
Sculpture in the Environment	(see SITE)	
Seagram Building	54	
Sears Tower	54	
Segal, Walter	51	
Semper, Gottfried	39	

Shanghai World Financial Centre	55	
Sheerness Navy Dockyard	43	
SITE	56	
Skidmore, Louis	54, 55	
Sony Building	(see AT&T Building)	
Soufflot, Jacques-Germain	36	
Sphinx, The	11	
St Basil's Cathedral	26	
St Pancras Hotel	37	
St Paul's Cathedral	34	
St Peter's Basilica	15, 23, 24, 31, 32, 34	
St Peter's Piazza	24, 32	
St-Etienne Church	18	
Staal, J.F.	49	
State Capitol	36	
Statue of Liberty, The	45, 46	
Stent, Thomas	37	
Step Pyramid, The	12, 29	
Stephenson, Robert	42, 44	
Stern, Robert	56	
Stirling, James	56	
Stonehenge	10	
Street, George Edmund	37	
Street, Peter	27	
Suleiman's Mosque, The	26	
Sullivan, Louis	47	
Sydney Opera House, The	53	
Tacoma Building	47	
Taipei 101	55	
Taj Mahal	35	
Tate Modern Gallery	57	
Teatro del Mondo	56	
Teatro Olimpico	25	
Telford, Thomas	42	
Tempietto di San Pietro	22, 24	
Temple at Karnak, The	12	
Temple Mayor	28, 29	
Temple of the Sun	29	
Tenochtitlan	29	
Teotichuacan	28	
Theatine Church in Munich, The	33	
Theatre at Sabrantha, The	14	
Tilt Showroom	56	
Tomb of Agammemnon, The	10	
Tour San Fins	55	
Tower of Babel, The	11	
Town Hall in Amsterdam, The	33	
Town Hall in Antwerp, The	25	
Town Hall in Hilversum, The	49	
Town Hall in Vicenza, The	26	
Trajan's Column	14, 31	
Treasury of Atreus, The	10	
Tribune Building	46	
Troja Palace	33	

Turin Cathedral	30	
U.N. Secretariat Building	54	
U.S. Pavilion	53	
Unité d'Habitation	51	
University Library at Charlottesville, The	37	
Utzon, Jorn	53	
Vanbrugh, John	34	
Vanna Venturi House	56	
Vau, Louis le	33	
Venturi, Robert	56	
Versailles Palace	(see Palace of Versailles, The)	
Vignola, Giacomo	22	
Vignon, Alexandre-Pierre	37	
Villa Farnesina	23, 24	
Villa Godi	24	
Villa Rotonda	22, 23, 25, 36	
Villa Savoye	51	
Von Erlach, Johann Fischer	31	
Votivkirche	38	
Wagner, Otto	48	
Walker Warehouse	47	
Wang, C.P.	55	
Wembley Stadium	57	
West Jackson Boulevard Building	47	
Western Union Telegraph Building	46	
Westminster Abbey	38	
Westminster Hall	38	
White House, The (original)	41	
White Temple, The	10	
Wichita House	51	
Wilford, Michael	56	
Winslow House	47	
Wood, John	36	
Woolworth Building	46	
World Trade Center, The	54, 55	
Wren, Christopher	34	
Wright, Frank Lloyd	47, 52, 54	
Yamasaki, Minoru	54	
Zigguarat Temple at Ashur, The	11	
Ziggurat of Etemenanki, The	(see Tower of Babel, The)	
Zuccali, Enrico	33	
Zwinger Palace	31	